PRAISE FOR *TOUGH GUYS AND DRAMA QUEENS*

"Mark's ministry overflows with biblical wisdom and practical insights gained over three decades of helping other parents like us. His impact on my own family has been measureable and lasting. Implement his insights and God's blessing will be increasing yours and your children's."

—DR. JAMES MACDONALD
WALK IN THE WORD RADIO PROGRAM
SENIOR PASTOR OF HARVEST BIBLE CHAPEL

"These are tough times for teenagers, and Mark Gregston offers a rare blend of humor, heart, and biblical wisdom."

—DR. JOHN TRENT
PRESIDENT, THE CENTER FOR STRONG FAMILIES
AUTHOR OF *THE BLESSING*

"Mark Gregston understands teens and their parents like very few in the world. This is the book I have been waiting for to give to parents when they tell me they just can't figure out what's going on with their teenager. Mark will help you navigate the ever changing teen culture as well as provide for you a very healthy parenting strategy. It's one of the best books on this subject I have ever read."

—JIM BURNS, PH.D.
PRESIDENT, HOMEWORD
AUTHOR OF *TEENOLOGY* AND *THE PURITY CODE*

"Mark Gregston is a parent's best friend in *Tough Guys and Drama Queens*. He takes parents into their teens' everyday reality and graciously shows them what they are doing wrong. I wrote in the margins throughout the book—a sign I *really* love a book!"

—BRENDA GARRISON
AUTHOR OF *LOVE NO MATTER WHAT*

"Mark shares his secrets to survival and success in raising teenagers, offering parents a hand as they struggle for help."

—STEVE LARGENT
FORMER U.S. CONGRESSMAN
MEMBER OF PRO FOOTBALL HALL OF FAME

"Mark has a clear 'big picture' grasp of effective parenting. It's formatted by the power of God's grace and seasoned from decades of experience."

—DR. TIM KIMMEL
PRESIDENT OF FAMILY MATTERS
AUTHOR OF *GRACE-BASED PARENTING*

"Mark refuses to pull any punches or sidestep any difficult situations. He speaks directly to the issues."

—JOE WHITE
PRESIDENT OF KANAKUK KAMPS

TOUGH GUYS

>>>>> AND <<<<<

DRAMA QUEENS

HOW NOT TO GET BLINDSIDED BY
YOUR CHILD'S TEEN YEARS

MARK L. GREGSTON

THOMAS NELSON
Since 1798

NASHVILLE   DALLAS   MEXICO CITY   RIO DE JANEIRO

Published in Nashville, Tennessee, by Thomas Nelson. Thomas Nelson is a registered trademark of Thomas Nelson, Inc.

Thomas Nelson, Inc. titles may be purchased in bulk for educational, business, fund-raising, or sales promotional use. For information, please e-mail SpecialMarkets@ThomasNelson.com.

Library of Congress Cataloging-in-Publication Data

Gregston, Mark, 1955-
  Tough guys and drama queens : how not to get blindsided by your child's teen years / Mark L. Gregston.
      p. cm.
  Includes bibliographical references (p.   ).
  ISBN 978-0-8499-4729-2 (trade paper)
  1. Parenting--Religious aspects--Christianity. 2. Child rearing--Religious aspects--Christianity. 3. Parent and teenager--Religious aspects--Christianity.
4. Church work with teenagers. I. Title.
  BV4529.G7337 2012
  248.8'45--dc23

                            2012003893

Printed in the United States of America

13 14 15 16 QG 9 8 7 6 5 4 3

To my mom,
Patricia Joanne Gregston
July 23, 1930—April 3, 2012

Contents

CONTENTS

Acknowledgments

Many people have contributed to this book either through influence, encouragement, or their sharing of insight. I'm thankful to all and especially grateful to the following folks:

Thanks to the Heartlight Ministries Foundation board of directors for your friendship, participation, and support of all the crazy ideas I share with you about helping more and more families across North America.

I am grateful for those at Heartlight; Blake Nelson, my son-in-law; and all the Heartlight Ministries staff who provide a setting of hope for parents in need. And I'm especially grateful for Ben Weinert, Corry Boatwright, and Meredith Grausam, the lightning rods of Heartlight. Thanks to our counselors at Heartlight—Justin Arnold, Rachel Olshine, Melodye Cure, Robert McGowen, and Melissa LeCraw; you've kick-started my thinking several times.

A special thanks to members of the Heartlight Ministries board of directors—Krista and Dan Darr, Jonathan and Jillian Greifenkamp, Joe and Jana Crawford, Mike and Dianne Puls, Raymond and Cindy Russell, John and Amy Hull, and Mike and Carol Barry. Your commitment to families is saving the lives of many.

Thank you, Sam Sheeley and Shane Goswick, whom I have the joy of working with every day.

My love and gratitude for Melissa Nelson, Amber Horton,

and Courtney Goswick are beyond words. Your commitment to be that "voice of hope" for so many inspires me.

I am appreciative of all the radio groups that carry our *Parenting Today's Teens* radio program. Your partnership with us spreads a message of help and hope to the desperate and desolate parents searching for assistance with their teens. Thank you to American Family Radio, Bott Radio, Christian Satellite Network, Moody Radio, and all those stations that carry our daily and weekend programs.

Very few people in this world are as blessed to have such encouraging friends as Bill and Susanne Walsh, Roger and Lori Kemp, Jerry and Leanne Heuer, and James and Kathy MacDonald, and George and Livia Dunklin. I love you guys.

This project would not have happened without the help of Robert Wolgemuth and Associates and in particular, Erik Wolgemuth. Thanks for your help, your patience, and your encouragement. And for Debbie Wickwire of Thomas Nelson, I am most grateful.

And last, but certainly not least, a hug-filled thanks to my wife of thirty-seven years, Jan. Your love and encouragement is beyond words.

>>> Introduction <<<

What Duck Hunting Taught Me about Adolescence

I swam competitively for years and even received a full-ride swimming scholarship to the University of Arkansas. I never thought I would come close to death by drowning. Until one fateful duck hunt.

You see, every year I take a group of guys to Arkansas to spend a couple of days duck hunting. Each morning we wake early, put on waders, grab our guns, and head out to wander through waist-deep water in search of the airborne delicacies that we hope will fly close enough to us that we can take them back to the hunting lodge as our afternoon snack.

On this particular morning, I slipped out of the boat into the calm, frigid water. The lake was no more than three feet deep, and I leaned against a tree hoping that my bulky clothing and the tree's bark would camouflage my presence. That way, I could surprise at least one of the millions of ducks that pass through the Mississippi migration flyway.

Expert swimmer. Good hunter. Shallow water. No big deal.

I spotted one and took a shot. My targeted duck made a splash, and I started to wade through the murky water to retrieve it. My focus was on the duck, my gun was in my hand, and I was determined to bag my first bird of the morning. It looked like it was going to be an easy task.

It rapidly proved otherwise.

With one foot cautiously following the other, I soon realized I was wading through toppled tree limbs, brush, thickets, and broken branches. Still I trudged on, convinced I knew what I was doing. Suddenly I tripped on something I hadn't seen in front of me. My foot wedged between two submerged logs, and my effort to pull it out threw me off-balance. As my left side slowly started to tilt into the water, I resolutely tried to keep my eyes focused on the duck (so as not to lose it) and my right hand out of the water (so I wouldn't lose my gun). In a split second, horror stories came to mind of how many a good hunter had drowned when his waders filled with water. Then the sensation of icy, cold water trickling down my back, covering my waders, woke me to the realization that I was going under. I needed to react quickly or the situation was going to go from bad to worse in a heartbeat.

My focus on something I thought was important (the duck) and my determination to hold on to something I thought was valuable (my gun) were causing me to sink. I had to rethink what was important or it was going to be the death of me. I grabbed a tree with my left arm and thrust my gun under the water with my right, in order to get my balance. As water poured into my waders, I took my focus off the all-important duck, rethought the value of my gun, and embraced something that was secure enough to save my life—the tree. This cold-water experience got my attention.

As soon as I evaluated what was truly important (my life) and let go of what wasn't (the duck and my gun), I was able to loosen my foot, regain my balance, stand up, and take a deep breath. My heart was pounding, my eyes were misty, and my back was wet. As I leaned against that tree, I exhaled a sigh of relief.

The Cold-Water Experience of Parenting Teens

My near-drowning duck-hunting experience on that cold, wet morning reminds me of the situations many, many parents of tweens and teens find themselves in every day. I've met hundreds of happy, loving moms and dads who waded blithely through their children's elementary years and then found themselves floundering in treacherous waters when their kids entered adolescence.

Parenting in the early years can be wonderful. It's full of hugs and kisses and accolades. Kids love their parents, and they tell them so. Fathers get T-shirts that say, "World's Greatest Dad," and mothers get coffee mugs that say, "I love you, Mom!" Parents may begin to coast along as the waters of adolescence approach. Well-meaning moms and dads overestimate their parenting abilities and underestimate the influence of the submerged "branches and logs" of cultural pressure that entangle their family when the teen years arrive.

These waters look calm and relatively safe, but there are many dangers just under the surface. As you began walking through these waters, you probably encountered a cold-water experience. A teenage daughter became mean, irate, or seductive in her demeanor. A once-engaging son became distant and despondent. Maybe your adolescent started experimenting with drugs or alcohol, got caught looking at porn, or traded in his good friends for some not-so-good new ones. Maybe your child now likes things he used to hate and hates things he used to like.

Other parents around you have teens who seem to be doing

well, and all of a sudden you doubt your parenting approach. You begin asking questions like, "How can this happen to us?" "She was such a good girl, wasn't she?" "Where did we go wrong?" or "What in the world is he thinking?"

A feeling like you are about to drown comes over you when a daughter comes home and announces that she's pregnant. Or a son comes home drunk. Or a policeman knocks at the door grasping your seemingly perfect child, who doesn't seem so perfect anymore. Maybe your waders began to fill when your not-so-little girl let you know she doesn't believe the things you've taught her, doesn't like you anymore, and doesn't think she needs you as a parent any longer. Perhaps it's your son telling you that he doesn't have to listen to you, all the while making sure you hear his angry rants and disrespectful comments. You may feel like you are going under for sure when you discover your child has been sexting pictures of herself to her boyfriend, or you find unacceptable language in your son's Facebook status updates, texts, or overheard conversations.

Experiences like these get your attention quickly, don't they? It's like someone pouring ice water down your back. If you've been there, you know exactly what I'm talking about. And if you haven't, chances are you hope you never will. But almost every parent will experience a dunking at some point in their children's adolescence; some will see their families nearly drown. And all of us, as parents, need to learn when to let go of what used to be important in order to cling to the true lifelines in the teen years.

Parents of tweens and teens need to hope for the best, prepare for the worst, and be proactive and effective in training our children to face the snares of adolescence. It's a time when a parent's naiveté can have enormous consequences, and overconfidence can leave you unprepared if your child should stumble and begin to go under.

Preparing for the Teenage Years

Most parents have some sort of plan for raising their children and think they are prepared. I made a plan for my duck hunt and thought I was prepared. I was a seasoned hunter. I felt, like many parents feel, like I had done it all before and was competent enough to handle anything that might come my way. When I got out of the boat and stepped into the water, I felt a great sense of confidence that it was going to be a great, successful day. I had walked through duck-hunting water before. But I had never walked in *this* water before.

When I started to wade through unfamiliar territory, that's when the trouble came. I didn't understand what lay beneath the calm waters. In many ways, that is just what it's like for parents entering their child's adolescent years for the first time. They just don't know what's hiding below the surface. And when their child's foot gets trapped by the culture, addictions, or dangerous behaviors they didn't see coming, many parents don't know how to pry it loose. Soon, the entire family may be in over its head.

My hope is that this book will prepare parents of younger children for what's lurking under the murky waters of adolescence before you step out of the elementary boat. It is also a tool to help parents already in the waters of the teenage years to help their children wade through adolescence without getting ensnared. Finally, my prayer is that this book will provide hope and a lifeline to parents who are already knee-deep in the muck with your tweens and teens.

It wasn't easy to pry my foot loose on that fateful day, and I had to let go of something valuable to do it. As parents, you may have to let go of some of your expectations and your plans in order to refocus on the big picture of what is truly important in order to preserve your family and your relationship with your child.

Before they entered their teenage years, academics, the way your children dress, the words they use, the views they take, or the comments they make might have been the most important areas you set your sights on correcting. Similarly, I thought bagging a duck was important; after all, it was a duck-hunting trip. But that duck, one of thousands, wasn't really important in comparison to saving my life.

Perhaps your parenting focus has been on the "bagging the duck" of managing your child's outward behavior when, in fact, your child's life desperately needs to be saved. For example, maybe you've had your heart set on your daughter becoming a great piano player, encouraging her to excel, and pushing her to practice. She is learning piano, but what you may have failed to notice is that she is also experimenting with drugs after school. Or you've been cheering your son at football, dreaming about him getting a college scholarship, unaware that he has started using steroids and is experiencing violent mood swings. I had to let go of my treasured gun to save myself. What might you need to let go of to save your child?

When a child stumbles and begins to go under because of the influence of the culture in which he is immersed, he needs parents who will shift their attention and efforts to what is truly important. I hope this book will show you ways to do just that. Because I don't want your son or daughter to experience what Megan did.

A Near-Drowning in a Cultural Tidal Wave

Through Heartlight Ministries, a residential counseling center for teens and their families,[1] I counseled Megan for over a year. She was a girl who grew up in a home with great parents, wonderful siblings, and an encouraging church family. Megan went to church every time the doors were open. She loved her brothers and sister, her parents, church, and friends. She made excellent grades, played every sport offered, and got along with all her teachers. When she was sixteen, she tried out for varsity cheerleader, and her mom threw a congratulatory party for all the girls who made the squad.

The newfound attention made Megan popular, and it wasn't long before she gained the attention of a lot of guys. The influence of a permissive and seductive culture quickly transformed this sweet little girl. She became a casualty of the cultural tsunami that swallowed her up and spat her out a mess. Megan's parents saw signs that all was not going well, but they thought she was just going through a phase. Their cold-water experience came when they discovered text messages on Megan's phone that indicated she was having sex with her boyfriend.

Megan's church friends found out and the word spread quickly in her youth group. What had been a place of welcome became a den of judgment. Even the cheerleading sponsor thought it was best not to have Megan cheer anymore. In just a few days, this once happy-go-lucky girl lost hope, felt rejected by her friends, and retreated from everyone as guilt and shame destroyed all the confidence she had.

Her parents were disappointed, of course. Their first response was to ground her for life and shame her for violating their family standards. Megan told me that her dad's first comment upon finding out was, "Every time I look at you I get sick thinking about what you have done." Her dad was infuriated and embarrassed, while her mom became ashamed and confused. Both withdrew from each other and felt alone in their social circle, where problems were better off left alone. Their attitude was, "Let's keep this to ourselves," leaving Megan nowhere to turn.

I remember Megan telling me, "My parents were so concerned about doing what they thought was right, they never asked me what was wrong."

This family found themselves submerged in a culture that had stolen their daughter's innocence. It was evident to me that if they didn't change their focus, let go of some things they had thought were important, and grab hold of some new ways to approach their sweet Megan, their relationship with their daughter was going to drown.

Becoming a Safe Harbor in Turbulent Teenage Years

Through Heartlight Ministries—a Christian residential center for troubled teens—I've spent the last thirty-eight years of my life helping teens like Megan and their parents get to better places in their relationships with each other. In that time, I've found that the needs of kids haven't changed, but their world has. Unless parents shift their approach to accommodate these changes and the resulting effects upon their adolescent, the turbulent waters ahead might just take the child or the parents under, no matter how strong they think they are at swimming. In Megan's situation, there were important steps her parents could have taken to bring this family back into better relationship with each other. They could have realized the effect the culture was having on their daughter and changed their approach to her. They could have understood that their daughter was more lost than intentionally rebelling and moved back toward her relationally. And they could have embraced a new style of parenting that prepared their child for life and saved her from her own demise. By grabbing on to these certain lifelines, they could have recognized this crisis as temporary turbulence in the bumpy ride of adolescence and responded to it in a healthy way.

In this book I will illuminate ways parents, like Megan's mom and dad, can better equip their children and themselves to face the teen years before they are upon them. If her parents knew what lay ahead and the right tools to clear the path, Megan's choices might have been different.

So the purpose of this book is twofold. First, to help parents better understand exactly what lies beneath the surface of the adolescent waters and to grasp the possible reasons that your child may fall or has already fallen into the snares of today's society. And second, to provide practical tools and tips to help parents abandon old-school parenting styles that aren't working and replace them with methods that engage your child in relationship. You can be a beacon of hope, a safe harbor in the turbulence of the teen years. I want to help you get there.

Be forewarned, there are treacherous waters ahead, but you and your child can ride the waves of the adolescent adventure together—and come out stronger. You may not get a duck, and it may cost you a few things you once thought were valuable. But in the long run, you can counteract the devastating effects of a culture steeped in evil, secure the safety of your child, and preserve the relationships within your family by following the practical tips and principles described in this book.

And that's worth more than a million ducks.

>>> **Part One** <<<

What's So
Different about
Today's Culture?

1

Overexposure to Everything

When I first met Amy I thought that the introduction would be no different from any of the other twenty-five hundred teens who have lived with us in our residential program at Heartlight Ministries. She was like many of the other teens who have lived on our campus; great parents, loving home, solid upbringing, opportunities for travel and vacations galore, attended a good school, and active in youth group and church. But there was one difference that was hard to believe: she was just fourteen.

Amy looked a lot older than she actually was, but her eyes said differently. As her parents explained Amy's recent actions and decisions that had brought her to the point of needing to participate in our program, I watched Amy's response. Her head drooped, her eyes filled with tears, her chin quivered, and her face showed a hint of embarrassment as her mom and dad told me of her poor choices. It was easy to tell that she was scared and wasn't just some spoiled, rebellious kid who needed correction. She was a little girl who had been exposed to way too much for a girl her age—and overexposed to areas no parent wants their sons or daughters to even know about at such a young age.

Amy would have eventually been exposed to all the behaviors that brought her to us—alcohol, drug use, alternative lifestyles, her own sexuality—in due time, perhaps in her later teen years, during college, during her first job, or after she got married. But she had been "overexposed" to these things far too young, when she didn't have the maturity or responsible mind-set to navigate her way through these difficult areas. What fourteen-year-old does?

This overexposure was killing Amy. She later told me that if she had not come to Heartlight Ministries and spent time working through these issues while living on our campus, she thinks she would have been dead. Truth is, this overexposure is killing our teens . . . their hopes and aspirations, parent's desires for them, and keeping them from becoming the young men and women they have the potential to be.

Here's a story picture of what I think is happening to teens today.

Most parents have played a simple game of catch in the yard, tossing a ball with the gentleness and ease of allowing a child to learn new and needed skills to catch a ball. In time, the child is handed a bat and begins to learn to swing at the ball that is pitched ever-so-easy to ensure that they connect the bat with the ball. It's an easy game that is usually full of laughter and joy as a child learns to hit what has been pitched to him or her.

Now here's what overexposure looks like.

A child is standing ready to take a chance to swing and hit something that is being pitched. As she stands with anticipation and excitement that she'll be able to "knock it out of the park," she smiles ear-to-ear for the new experience to earn the applause and cheering of parents, siblings, and grandparents.

But instead of that gentle toss of a ball that matches her age-appropriate ability to hit with a bat, multiple balls start flying toward her with an intensity that is far above her ability to swing or her agility to get out of the way. As a continual barrage of balls pelts her, her lovable smile quickly turns to tears. The last thing on her mind now is hitting a ball; she is only thinking of self-preservation and protection, turning away from something she thought would be fun and hiding from the onslaught of pain that keeps coming. What was to be this child's next step, taken with applause from those around her, has turned into a nightmare that eventually breaks the heart of this little girl who thought she was ready to take her first swing.

Because of the pain of overexposure, the little girl's innocence coming into the opportunity was lost. She is now not quite as trusting as she once was when others want to pitch her a ball. She's weary and hesitant to step up to the plate. She feels like a failure, a loser, and one who won't ever be able to live up to people's expectations. So she withdraws, gives up hope, leans on her own understanding of her small world, and swears she'll never trust or get hurt again. Her new behaviors are now aimed at filling her losses, compensating for her embarrassment, and keeping her pain from happening again.

This is what overexposure looks like. This type of response is what I saw on Amy's face the first time I met her.

Amy is not unlike many other teens. She is growing up in a culture that exposes our children to influences that are counter to what most parents want deeply for their child. Adolescents today would have to be completely isolated to avoid the culture's power to affect and sway their moral judgment. And you and I know it—most of us have commented about how glad we are not to have to grow up in today's teen culture. Our teens are victims of this culture and they feel its impact every day. And if parents don't change their parenting style to withstand the effects of the current cultural influence, I fear our teens will leave the batter's box, abandoning the values and principles that parents hoped to instill in their children.

Here are some areas of overexposure that shape the way our kids think, act, and perceive the truths their parents present to them.

Information Bombardment

The vast amount of written information swells at an increasing rate every day. In the 1930s, written information doubled every thirty years. In the 1970s and 1980s, that amount of information doubled every eleven years. Today, codified information doubles every eleven hours. That means that you can end your workday being half as wise as you were when you woke up that morning![1] The amount of information available today far exceeds one's ability to contain it all. Intellectual prowess is now defined not by one's capacity to retain information, but by one's ability to search and find information.

How does this affect kids today?

Where there used to be one answer from research, there are now many to choose from. There isn't just one encyclopedia on the shelf that will give an answer to questions; there are hundreds and hundreds of resources online that provide answers at a click of a mouse.

In response to this barrage of data, many teens are wondering, *Which source is correct? Who should I trust? With so much to pick from, which do I choose? My parents are not the only source of wisdom and answers. If I don't like one answer, I can find another. I can find information to justify whatever I want to believe.*

Overexposure of Images and Words

The explosion of the number of videos and photos available to our teens is astronomical, and digital photography has placed cameras in everyone's hands. So many activities and habits that were once unseen are now viewed publicly, and competition to post images of trysts, travels, and talents has created a world of social networking where imagery and bragging rights are the measures of one's value and influence.

Facebook currently has 250 million pictures uploaded each day, and growing daily.[2] There are over 4.2 million pornographic sites on the Internet.[3] YouTube contains over 80 billion videos.[4] And 69 percent of American heads of households play computer and video games.[5] With these ever-growing statistics, I can't help but wonder how we spend our time. Anything viewed or spoken has influence. And influence that once came from relationships and trusted friends has now been superseded by imagery and voyeurism, and from attention-seeking and self-promoting acquaintances.

Profanity that was once taboo in society is now commonplace and widely accepted. (Why, if I had said things to my dad that I hear teens saying to theirs today, I would have been knocked halfway into next week!) Abusive and obscene song lyrics, televised images of violence and death, and videos of once-forbidden topics and illicit images have not only invaded our information and entertainment systems, but they have changed the social standard of acceptance. The offensive, unthinkable, and unmentionable are no longer off-limits, and the boundaries of images and words have been so expanded that very few blush or turn their heads in embarrassment when encountered.

And the effect of this seismic shift of values on teens? It has changed the world we live in, even if our kids don't understand or acknowledge the differences in the world they are growing up in and the one you and I did. Their world is different, so their responses are different. What was abnormal to our generation has become their normal. What was unacceptable to us has become acceptable to them. Our blushing has become their humor. Because of repeated overexposure, teens have become numb to images and words that once aroused and offended people. They don't understand why parents make such a big deal over something that, in their world, is ordinary. They dislike when parents question their standards and interpret their parents' attempt to curb their digital intake and verbal output as an effort to curb their social interaction.

Sexualization of a Culture

Sex sells. It entices, it attracts, and it has an amazing appeal to disconnected girls who desire to have someone pay attention to them and to confused young men who long for ways to express their manhood. And in a world of pornographic influence, prominent images, media stimuli, and marketing schemes, a permissive culture is created where seduction is a fad and exploring one's sexual curiosity is encouraged. Abstaining from or delaying sexual interactions is discouraged in a culture in which the invitation to participate has been replaced by an expectation to be involved.

Another effect of this constant sexual exposure in the life of kids is that their curiosity is piqued, often causing them to experiment sexually at an earlier age. The perfect storm has formed where middle school guys exposed to porn and middle school girls confronting their sexuality has collided, and the dark clouds of sexual experimentation have eliminated the sunshine of innocence, causing kids to grow up way too soon. The resulting storm damage caused by this early overexposure is that sexual activity confuses and clouds thinking patterns at an early age.

Too often, well-intentioned parents give in to the culture's sexual permissiveness. Well-meaning parents, in their attempt to make sure their child fits in or isn't eliminated from social circles, sometimes allow sexualized music, style of clothing, videos, and discussions to trump modesty, sexual boundaries, and moral standards. It seems as though many kids who grew up in the 1980s and were told to "Just say no!" are having a hard time shifting the application of that phrase to their parenting style.

Granted, in country terms, it's "a tough row to hoe" for parents to balance a child's need to have friends with the child's desire to maintain moral principles and modesty in the process. It's an especially hard path for kids to walk when parents permit an anything-goes mentality to erode their own parental influence.

Whenever parents or teens embrace the mind-set that one's physical appearance and sexuality are a measure of their value, then the true desires of the heart are missed and emptiness is filled with unhealthy pursuits that take teens down a path that is usually met with a dead end—or worse.

And here's what I encountered with my fourth-grade granddaughter—it starts early.

I love spending time with my grandchildren. Their innocence, the beauty of their laughter, and their childlike joy have an amazing way of making my heart jump when they call out "Papa!" It's the same feeling I get when they send me texts telling me how much they love me, or when they leave messages on my phone to ask how I'm doing and end with "I love you!" It's sweet, but even this grandpa knows that eventually a shift will occur in my young grandchildren's life signaling an end to their innocence and usher in a more challenging time that is the next stage of life.

I'm blessed to have my grandkids live close by. The older one in fourth grade, Maile, asked me to bring her lunch and eat with her at her school so that she could consume something other than what was being served at the school cafeteria. She also wanted me to meet one of her teachers who had read some of my books and wanted to show me her world. It was a time that I simply consider sweet. So this fifty-six-year-old grandpa decided to enter her fourth grade world, as I wasn't about to miss this opportunity.

As I was leaving the school, she gave me a hug, told me she loved me, and asked if I could pick her up after school to get an ice cream cone. The beauty of the moment felt like a slow-motion movie. Then, out of left field, I was blindsided by a young classmate of Maile's who ran up and yelled inquisitively, "Hey, Maile! Do you want to have sex with Chad?" In that moment, I wanted to do something to that punk that I never think about unless I'm on a hunting trip. She was embarrassed, he ran off, and my blood began to boil. I asked her, "That happen often?" She just sighed loudly. Needless to say, it gave us something to talk about that day over ice cream.

I indeed walked on her turf that day. Now in fifth grade, Maile's world is a mixture of two influences: one that has been created by her parents, and one that is being sculptured by powers outside her home. One world of the sweet innocence of life is beginning to bash up against this world of exposure. The conflict between these worlds has begun and I don't think she even knows it. Perhaps that's why older folks enjoy the goodness and purity of those pre-middle-school years so much and take advantage of every chance to spend time touching a life unscathed by the cruelness of the world.

Now I'm not an anti-world kind of guy. I do believe that evil exists, but I also believe that the good guys eventually win. I also believe in Satan and his influence, but I don't see demons and oppression around every corner. I understand the nature of sin and equally understand the depravity of man. But I love this world, and I love those in it. And all the stuff (a simple term that could be expressed more accurately with barnyard slang) that is encountered is just that—stuff that we, as parents, need to help our children navigate through the cultural jungle of complexity and confusion. My granddaughter, like all other fifth graders, now has awareness of that other world of influence and will soon become conscious that a new set of skills is required to help her steer through the maze of choices in middle school and throughout her high school years.

That world that once only consisted of riding bikes, nature hikes, playing with a dog, drawing chalk pictures on the driveway, dancing in the living room, coloring pictures worthy of hanging on the refrigerator, watching cartoons, doing gymnastics, playing on soccer teams, and having her first experience on a plane, at the beach, or staying at a hotel, has shifted gears. My prayer for my granddaughter is no different from the prayers of every other parent and grandparent who has kids this age: that she would survive the upcoming years with relationships intact with me, with God, and with great friends. And I pray that she would be prepared for the life that is laid before her.

My anger aimed at the young man who blindsided me was misplaced. My angst should not have been directed toward him, as he was also a victim of a culture that was spewing venom all over our young people. If anger is an emotional response to not getting what one wants, then my feelings that day were more centered on something that I wanted . . . and what I didn't want. At the core of my frustration, I didn't want things to change for my granddaughter. And at the heart of that core, I didn't want the world to change for me. That change meant that a new stage of life was beginning and what was to come would require more of me in my relationship with Maile. That afternoon, between the time of eating lunch at her school and having an ice cream cone following a day of learning, something changed. And what changed was me. I realized that now that she not only *wanted* to spend time with me; she *needed* to spend time with me to help her maneuver through the new world she was entering.

The culture that you and I observe our preteens and teens living in today is far different than the one you and I grew up in. And I'll bet you've thought what so many parents (and grandparents) have pondered: *I'm glad I don't have to grow up in today's teen culture.* It's tough. It's confusing. And it can have some pretty dramatic and life-controlling consequences.

Influences on Children Who Are No Longer Controlled by Parents

Parents used to be the gatekeepers of information allowed into a home and the ones who would determine the exposure their children would have to various topics, guiding them at age-appropriate times to face current issues. Parents determined what was acceptable and what was not for their children.

Even in today's culture, parents must not only assume but exercise their right of parenting for the benefit and protection of their children. In a culture that prematurely distributes information and ignores long-held principles of appropriateness, restraint, and permissible exposure, parents must stand firm about allowing these influences into their home. Otherwise, the culture's invasion into our homes is like a bull in a china shop that cares little about the damage his actions are doing and doesn't understand the adverse influence he can have on the delicate and fragile hearts of children.

As I have mentioned, too many times parents allow the culture to determine the level of appropriateness for our kids. So parents must understand the exposure their kids succumb to in their public world of school and, more importantly, in the private area of their Internet access and social networking.

Permission for Alternatives

Adolescence is a time that curiosity is piqued, and the natural questioning of a tween is replaced by the teen exploration mind-set of, "Let's do it!" This is a natural part of adolescence. But it's a dangerous part when so many offerings are before a teen hungry for excitement, experimentation, and interaction with others. Couple these desires with a culture where alternatives are prominent, permissible, and promoted, and it becomes another potentially turbulent ride for parents.

The dissemination of certain information to experience-seeking teens many times opens the door to new opportunities, new ways of expressing identity, and another chance to impress or engage with friends on a new level.

More potent drugs and harder alcohol are easier to attain in our permissible society. A teen's search for identity and expression has been enhanced by tattoos, piercings, unusual hair color or shaved heads, and outlandish clothing styles. The National Center for Health Statistics reported in 2011 that 30 percent of girls and 35 percent of guys between the ages of fifteen and seventeen had engaged in oral sex.[6] Even scarier, The Journal of Adolescent Health reported, "In all, 54% of adolescent females and 55% of adolescent males have ever had oral sex."[7] Today, the door has been opened for teens to engage in same-sex relationships. In the same study mentioned above, 10.6 percent of girls between the ages of fifteen and nineteen had engaged in some sort of same-sex contact.[8] Now that may not seem like too high of a percentage, 1 in 10. And it's not . . . unless that "1" is your daughter.

The Internet has changed the way kids learn about these new coping habits. If it can be displayed on the Internet, through videos, or mentioned on Facebook, then new behaviors are explored. Some of these are fantasy games, where a person can "get lost" in another world, temporarily leaving the stress and pressure of their current world (the same holds true about porn). Self-harm (such as cutting) has become a well-known coping activity among teens when ten years ago, it was hardly mentioned in adolescent circles. Another behavior is the potentially deadly "choking game," where a person self-strangulates in order to achieve a brief high that results from oxygen rushing back to the brain after it's been temporarily cut off. Videos about "huffing" gasoline, aerosols, Freon from air conditioners, and cleaners are widely available online, as well as information about "pharm parties," where each kid brings some type of prescription drug from home, mixes theirs with others, and then all participate in the tasting. And the use of bath salts to get high is based on the assumption that if it's legal to purchase, then it must be safe. Internet sources are abuzz about the way that one can get high by snorting or smoking nutmeg, a household cooking spice. If any new high or a new coping mechanism can be talked about or shown in a video, you can bet normal teenage curiosity, coupled with new alternatives, leads many to an opportunity for experimentation.

Information has an amazing way of influencing teens, doesn't it? Whether it is the Internet, a tweet, a podcast, a YouTube video, a blog, or a Facebook discussion, kids are exposed to more ideas and thoughts that once embraced can spread like an East Texas wildfire.

Is this flow of information ever going to stop? Will our kids ever be less exposed in the days ahead? The answer is no. Because teens will always behave like teens, and the information flow will only increase, it's imperative for parenting styles to shift as rapidly as the changing cultural influences, making sure that the ever-fluctuating and unstable stimuli do not overshadow our desire and efforts for our kids to live a moral and principled life.

And Amy? She's doing fine. She's doing well because her parents stopped trying to stop all the exposure she was affected by and started learning how to counter the effects that overexposure was having on her life. They began to understand the world their daughter was living in; thus, they changed their approach to her and instigated a new model of parenting that I will discuss in the last section of this book. Her parents applied specific techniques to counter the effect the overexposure was having on her life.

Above all, I think Amy's parents learned this: the teen years for any kid these days aren't just a game of catch in the front yard. It's a time when our kids have been forced into the "big leagues"—where the balls are thrown harder and come faster—and parents need to teach kids how to swing well so they, like Amy, will survive their teenage years and learn how to knock it out of the park.

>>> 2 <<<

Lack of Real Connection

grew up in a time when it was a three-channel world. No, I'm
not talking about the three television channels of CBS, NBC,
and ABC back when you actually had to get up to change the
channel. I'm referring to the time in communication history when
most people transferred information through these three channels:
face-to-face conversation, a written letter, or a phone call (which
was usually limited to five or ten minutes, depending on the mood
of my parents that day).

Things have changed a bit, haven't they? Those three TV channels have turned into more than eight hundred cable channels. If
you don't like what you're watching, with a click of a button you
can find something else that amuses you. And the three channels
of engagement have expanded into countless forms of communication to converse and transfer information.

Teens today use Facebook, iPads, smart phones, texting,
Twitter, e-mail, YouTube, websites, blogs, RSS feeds . . . it makes
my head spin just thinking about all the ways they communicate,
the ways we all do. Yet the difference between how parents communicate and how teens today communicate is that most of us
still use the three-channel ways of communication *plus* all the new
ways . . . but teenagers don't.

Teens today rely on the short one-liners of texting to have a discussion. Many have become more intent about sharing what is happening to them than listening to what's happening to others. And parents hoping to have a long discussion with their teen find that conversation interrupted repeatedly by texts demanding an immediate response. Parents want to talk, but their kids just want to get it over with and get back to their world of technology.

Texting is big. No matter what number I give you as to national surveys that derive statistics on the numbers of teens texting, it will be outdated by the time this book is printed. Statistics show that 6.1 trillion texts were sent last year.[1] Over 72 percent of teens text.[2] That's over two hundred thousand texts a second.

The impact I see from this change in communication style is that teens today have so many forms of communication, and they communicate often, yet very few are making true connections with one another. It is this lack of connection with one another that is ushering in some big challenges in relationships within the teen culture and the way they engage with one another and with their parents.

I've always believed that each person has a natural desire to connect with other people. I believe that we were created as relational beings with a desire for friendship that shows itself in our wishes to be attached to people, to be joined in companionship and bonded by friendships that fill a void that can only be satisfied with interpersonal relationships. We all have a longing for belonging.

Teens' lack of genuine relationship with one another fuels their drive to connect, so they go to greater lengths to get noticed and make a statement in hopes that someone will pay attention to them. They come across like tough guys and drama queens in hopes of finding others that will value who they are and what they are about. In their desperation for attention and their pursuit of value, they have become a generation screaming, "Look at me!"

The greatest tragedy of this "look at me" generation is that the development of character has taken a backseat to the attitudes that are constantly displayed in today's teen culture, expressed through their communication, and supported in today's media. If anyone wants to know why teens today are more immature than teens of the same age years ago, all you have to do is look at the way they engage with one another. Here are three attitudes of today's teen culture that I believe are damaging a teen's development and pursuit of relationships with one another.

Expression Is Welcomed and Encouraged

If you listen to talk radio, you'll hear opinions expressed right and left. Turn on any news station and you'll hear just about every observation and insight you'll need for a lifetime.. There are afternoon talk shows, satellite radio, YouTube videos galore, millions of websites, and an overabundance of blogs where anyone can read opinions pertaining to just about anything anyone could think of. Everyone has an opinion and thinks it has to be heard, and they encourage others to believe that their opinions deserve to be heard too. I doubt many of us could go through the day without hearing loudly the feelings, views, thoughts, and ideas of others, even when we don't want to.

I can't help but be reminded of the proverb that says, "Fools . . . delight in airing their own opinions" (Proverbs 18:2 NIV). Everyone is entitled to his or her opinion, right? Sure. In the United States of America, we are free to express ourselves all the time. And people enjoy expressing themselves through tattoos and bumper stickers with messages, Facebook posts that leave me wondering why anyone would share such personal information with me, and blogs that answer the directive, "Tell me how you really feel." TMI (too much information) is a common text-message response to oversharing. With just one click of a post or text message, everyone else gets to see your cause, opinions, and perceptions.

It seems as though we've transitioned the emphasis in this culture from wanting to fit in to one where everyone is wanting to stand out. Standing out, being noticed by others, brings much needed attention and gives a unique chance to be valued. But when the desire to stand out is coupled with immaturity and irresponsibly expressing one's opinions, the risk of damaging relationships increases greatly because of the digital means to widely and instantly distribute thoughts, feelings, and attitudes.

Here's a problem with teens: the expression of opinions is usually, but not always, coupled with a hint of sarcasm. And with most sarcasm, there is someone who is the brunt of the mockery and cynicism. I anguish over this teen culture's attitude of judgment and meanness. When a teen bears the brunt of sarcasm, it can be very destructive. It's destructive not just because someone is having conflict with another person but when a conflict between two people is quickly expanded, through wide distribution where expression runs rampant, into a crusade of many teens against one.

In our residential counseling center I've lived with both types of teens—those who bully others and those who have been bullied. In the unbridled world of teen communication, sarcastic one-liners can quickly destroy the image, reputation, and character of the one who becomes the target of another teen's sarcasm. A vast audience can receive this digital sarcasm in milliseconds and allow new recipients the chance to participate in the conflict and express their thoughts on what should have been a private matter. What once was a conflict between two people quickly becomes an electronic wildfire that can destroy the heart of a teen in as much time as it takes to hit the Send button.

This intent to tear someone apart with a strong dose of digital bullying encourages public expression when a private face-to-face discussion is absent. It's a game of one-upmanship where digital drama draws attention, elevates the winner, and fulfills the desire to stand out so that one will be noticed. But it's a tough world for the one caught in the crosshairs of teen expression at its worst—and it's even harder for parents when the teen being bullied is one they know.

Appearance Is Priority

Relationships that consist only of shallow, impersonal conversation have to rely on something to draw people together. The result is that image becomes everything and first impressions become overly important. There's nothing new about teens wanting to be proud of their physical dress and appearance. The difference today is that so many feel they *need* to look good in order to be accepted by peers.

This is how the desire to fit in with cultural trends and the culture's definition of beauty fleshes out in the life of many teenagers you know:

- A daughter shows a little more skin and violates her standards of modesty to attract guys or to fit in with other girls her own age.
- Your best friend's son starts using language while texting or posting on social network sites that is unacceptable to parents but welcomed in a teen's world because he wants to appear to be strong, manly, and tough.
- Your pastor's son changes preferences in music and lifestyle because he wants to disconnect with a church group that has high moral expectations and connect with another group of friends who accept him for who he is.
- A twelve-year-old niece is being made fun of by her peers for the way she dresses and now wants new clothes, a new hairstyle, painted nails, and makeup, all to find acceptance by those who ridicule her.
- Your next-door neighbor's daughter takes advantage of her photography skills and sends seductive or scantily clad pictures of herself in hopes of finding a connection . . . with your son.

I would venture to say that all teen behavior is driven by the need to belong. Many teens who want to change their appearance do so to make up for the extreme emptiness felt relationally during the teen years. Even more of a priority than needing to look good in the sight of peers is the need for a real connection among peers. And that necessity is so strong today because of the void of fulfilling relationships, a void that many teens are so desperate to fill that they will violate years of character building by their parents to fill that emptiness.

Performance Is Crucial

Any teen's identity is wrapped up in a number of things. As we've seen so far in this chapter, teens' expression of their thoughts and their physical appearance are significant factors in fulfilling that longing for belonging when deeper relationships have exited the equation. The third element that has increased in importance for teens is that performance is crucial.

I enjoy watching the reality talent shows, such as *American Idol* and *America's Got Talent*. The part that I love the most is the selection process of people who will be allowed to compete at higher levels. I am amused at contestants who state, "I need this, so please send me through to the next level" with such fervor that it appears their very life depends on it. For many, I think it does. These contestants need to be valued on the basis of their performance, because their sense of value and self-worth is not coming from their peer relationships.

Many times, they've been deceived or lied to about how good they really are in a particular ability. I'm surprised that my granddaughters' soccer teams don't keep score because the coaches say, "We're all winners." And they give trophies to everyone on the team, because the coaches tell the kids, "We're all winners." When we as parents do this, we're setting up future times of confusion when a child loses and can't fulfill what he used to be when he was a winner. No wonder 37 percent of kids feel like they'll one day become a superstar.[3] What a shocking conclusion most of them will come to one day!

I fear that a parent's desire for his or her child to have a good self-image by not allowing them to lose or fail ends up postponing a true understanding of how the world operates. Eventually, a teen will have to accept failure. If parents don't allow the slow trickle of realization of failure at age-appropriate times, that harsh reality will confront them at a confusing time during middle school when their self-esteem is already being questioned.

So what does this look like in a teen culture, when performance is crucial?

- It's the daughter who will stop at nothing to make good grades and either immerse herself into studies or learn to cheat because she feels she has to do well in school to find her value in life.
- It's your son's best friend who will fulfill the dares or push the limits with drugs and alcohol, and engage in some unthinkable behavior because his friends pushed him into it.
- It's a young lady in your church's youth group having oral sex with a guy because sexual performance is vital to keeping the relationship.
- It's the girl who checked your groceries this morning at the local grocery store who is encouraged by her friends to have sexual intercourse because she needs to complete her "rite of passage" into their circle of friendships.
- It's the daughter who dives into depression and now hates her parents after realizing that she isn't as talented or gifted as her parents led her to believe.
- It's the teenager who performs obsessively in athletics, band, or academics because he's deriving his value and importance from his performance rather than his love of the pursuit of the game or his talent.

Here's the point of this chapter: Kids want to belong some-where. And because relationships don't offer a connection that is so desperately wanted, dependence on finding ways to stand out, appear right, and perform well become paramount.

I often think those kids (teen, tweens, and even those in their early twenties) who opt out of the influence of the teen cultural cir-cus can be the healthiest of the whole bunch. Concerned parents ask me about their child's overinvolvement with video games and movies, and many times I feel that their child has simply learned a way to escape the confusion of a culture that is so counter to what most parents want for their child. Their participation in video games becomes a coping skill that provides a place of escape and a respite from the craziness of this teen culture. While I don't always agree with the way in which they disengage, I sure understand why they separate.

Is it any wonder that anxiety among teens is on the rise? I'll talk about this further in chapter 4.

Parents often ask me to help them know how to counter the effects of this culture on their teen. Here is my answer: never has there been a greater need for relationships in the lives of our children. What your tween, teen, or young adult really needs is something only you can offer—your time, relationship, wisdom, and experience. As we'll explore more deeply in part 3, parents who commit to spend time with their children, building deep and lasting relationships with them, can greatly counter the effects this culture is having on them from preteen years all the way through young adulthood.

3

Overresponsible Parents, Irresponsible Kids

When I first met twenty-three-year-old Rachel, I was impressed with the way she presented herself and somewhat awestruck at her résumé, which detailed many outstanding qualities, experience she had to offer to our children's ministry, and some amazing goals that were in line with our mission to families. So I hired her.

I knew within a couple of months that I had made a terrible mistake. During that period of time I witnessed childish behavior and a gross absence of the verbal skills her résumé reported she possessed. She possessed an immaturity that was reflected in her inability to get work completed on time, follow through on projects, and complete tasks that were given to her. She was awkward in social settings, childish in peer relations, and had no respect for authority. She always had an excuse for unfinished tasks and justification for everything missed. Despite being in her early twenties, Rachel behaved like an immature high school girl who appeared ready for the job but was nothing like she described herself in the job interview.

At lunch one day, Rachel shared that her dad had written all her college papers and had crafted for her what he thought would be a good résumé to send to potential employers. Those at the table now knew the reason behind the frustrations we felt as we listened to her stories of how Rachel's dad had done everything for her. She thought it was funny. I thought it was sad. I found myself getting angry—not at her, but at her dad, who, in his well-intentioned assumption of his daughter's responsibilities, created a mess for our staff and a greater mess for her. This girl wasn't prepared for the world in which she was to function; instead, she was living in a fantasy world because an overresponsible parent had created an irresponsible young lady who quickly lost her job.

The Adolescent Years

The period between childhood and adulthood is called adolescence. It does include the teenage years, but the period of adolescence has expanded a few years earlier and a few years later. Some studies suggest that adolescence now ranges from ages ten to twenty-six. It's not just the teen years anymore. Since the period of adolescence now starts sooner and lasts longer, parents' training of preteens must also start earlier, and parenting influence (not irresponsibility) must remain in play longer. Social issues influence kids as young as ten, and those issues linger until they turn twenty-four.

It's during adolescence that kids are supposed to learn how to become independent, how to grasp the meaning of relationships with the opposite sex, how to build friendships, how become financially responsible, how to make good choices, how to respect those who don't deserve it, the value of a good day's work, and the concept that there are consequences for inappropriate and unacceptable behavior. They are to become comfortable in their own skin and develop healthy social skills that will serve them well when they leave home, go to college, start working, get married, or enter military service.

During this time, kids should develop certain capabilities so that they can become mature young adults, capable of acting and thinking as young adults. In this period of adolescence, a parent's role is critical and essential to their child's development. If a parent is not involved, a teen has to learn from others how to function in the world. If a parent is too involved, kids end up like Rachel. I would submit that somewhere between being overinvolved heli-copter parents who hover over a child's every waking moment and underinvolved parents who allow kids to roam like free-range chickens, there is a point of healthy involvement where the focus of your parenting is to help your teenagers develop responsibility for their lives.

The Progression of Parenting

Most parents strive to *please* a child during the first years of their life. Every time a child in the early years cries, gets a boo-boo, or says she needs something, parents run to make sure that need is met and will do anything to make the child "feel all better." That's how it's supposed to be.

When the child enters elementary school, parents shift to *pro-tecting* their child, which is a natural and healthy responsibility for parents of children who are young and dependent on others. Parents have to. If they didn't, children would end up killing themselves; falling off of something they shouldn't be on, drinking something they shouldn't drink, or playing with things they're not supposed to play with. The danger comes when parents begin to overprotect their child, thinking that if they don't the child won't live to see middle school.

When middle school rolls around, many parents make another shift to begin *providing* for their child, which again, can be a healthy stage of equipping a preteen to deal responsibly with money and possessions. However, some parents go beyond a healthy provision for their children into *overproviding* for their preteens, giving them more than they'll ever need and unwittingly feeding their natural selfishness.

In high school and beyond, parental responsibility shifts into *preparing* your children for adulthood. The problem is that many parents stay stuck in the *overproviding-overprotecting-overpleasing* stages and fail to shift to a style of *preparing* their adolescents. And in the absence of preparing, these parents continue to provide things that are never good enough to their teen, who feels entitled, wants the world to revolve around him (because it has for so many years), and is never happy with what he's given because there is always something better out there.

In this unhealthy parenting scenario, overprovision quickly moves to enabling. Well-intended parents who want to give everything to their kids often have no idea of the havoc this parenting style creates in their kids' lives, because they aren't around to see what happens when their teen moves on to an independent life. I really think the job at Heartlight Ministries was Rachel's first encounter with a world that demanded responsibility, and she couldn't reach the bar.

So if you write your child's papers in middle school, you'll write them in high school. And if you write them in high school,

I guarantee that you'll write them in college because your child, who's now nineteen years old, doesn't know how to write a paper because you have been *overresponsible* in providing rather than responsible in preparing.

Here are a few things that parents' overresponsibility does to teens who need to be prepared for their future life.

Overresponsible Parenting Stifles Motivation

If all behavior is goal oriented, and the goals are already being met by parents who assume the responsibility to give, do, and be everything to their child, then there's no reason for behavior that is intended to meet the goals. If a dad always cleans up a child's messes, then there's no reason for a child to clean up after himself. If a mom always brings food to her child, then there's no reason for a child to learn to cook and provide for himself. If a well-meaning mom always does the laundry, homework, cooking, and picks out her daughter's clothes, then that young lady will smell bad, flunk out of school, eat unhealthily, and not be able to dress herself. If a dad always speaks for his son, then his son will never learn to speak for himself. If a mom always answers every question that comes before her tween or teen, then there's no motivation for her daughter to search for the answer herself. And kids will let you do it.

Overresponsible Parenting Eliminates Creativity

The parable of the prodigal son is an amazing story (Luke 15:11–25 NIV). In this famous story, a rebellious son demands his portion of the inheritance from his father and leaves home to pursue a lifestyle of excess and immorality. He lives it up for a while—until he runs out of money, and his buddies abandon him. Alone and desperate, the prodigal son ends up feeding pigs to survive, and at one point is so hungry that he looks longingly at the pig slop. When he has finally hit rock bottom, the son comes to his senses and creates a plan to go home and seek reconciliation with his father.

You may have heard or read this story, but something many people miss in the parable is the verse right before the son "came to his senses" (v. 17). It's this: "no one gave him anything" (v. 16). When people quit helping him, the son finally came to his senses. It reminds me of the saying: "Necessity is the mother of invention." When the prodigal son ran out of options, he had to get creative. He came up a plan of how to reengage with the father he had offended and what he must do to make things right.

Overresponsible Parenting Promotes Irresponsibility

Parents who are quick to accept the responsibility of making sure their teen is happy, provided for, and protected from all potential harm, many times don't realize how their "overresponsibility" keeps the concept of responsibility from transferring to their child. This transfer of responsibility is so important because if a teen isn't held accountable to take control of their life then they remain overly dependent on parents.

With acceptance of responsibility comes maturity. And as a teen matures, he or she becomes more independent. But the opposite is true as well. With the rejection of responsibility comes immaturity. And when a teen remains immature, he or she remains dependent on others.

Parents naturally want to do things for their child, but if they never help their child learn to become mature and independent, the child will be lazy, bored, and remain in a selfish state of dependence on their parents—hardly what any parent really wants for their child. The only way a child develops the character trait of responsibility is by having someone give it to him.

The basic thought that runs through a child's mind that says, *If someone else is being responsible for me, then I don't have to be. So, as long as my mom and dad do everything, I don't have to do anything.*

Overresponsible Parenting Postpones Maturity

The longer a parent holds onto responsibilities that should be gradually transferred to a child to help him or her grow up, the longer it will take for that child to mature. Just as the by-product of gaining responsibility is maturity, the by-product of not gaining responsibility is irresponsibility.

So when a teen is unmotivated, irresponsible, and immature, many times the parents are overresponsible, overproviding, and overprotective. And the result is that the child will "fail to launch" and have a greater tendency to become a boomerang kid.

I call these parents who choose to micromanage and can't quite let a child assume responsibility for their life "curling parents." If you watch the Winter Olympics, you'll get a glimpse of the sport of curling. I'm not sure what the purpose of the sport is, but I watch in laughter as a team gives a polished stone a push and then hovers over the stone being pushed down the ice, sweeping everything out of the way, yelling encouragements to the stone to make sure that it gets to its destination. I wonder if parents who hover over their children like a curling match don't trust what they've taught their children.

Teens whose parents are overresponsible end up learning life lessons the hard way—at the expense of a job (like Rachel), a marriage, or even their own kids. Many get angry that their parents didn't prepare them for adulthood. The only option for many is to rebel so that a parent's role of overinvolvement stops.

Look, I live with sixty high school kids on our Heartlight campus. I understand what to expect from their thinking and what to anticipate in their behavior. No doubt, kids are more immature today than those the same age were fifteen years ago. But maturity isn't there many times because moms and dads are more bent to be a *peer-ent* than a *parent*, which enables their teen to continue in their adolescent mind-set and immature behavior.

Will You Keep Rescuing Your Child?

Parents, you have an important decision to make: will you keep rescuing your child from life by assuming too much responsibility for your child's life, or will you help your child develop muscle for the tough tasks that lie ahead of every teen?

Adolescents whose parents carefully and gradually place a mantle of age-appropriate responsibility will progressively take ownership of their values and actions, mature, develop healthy social interactions and personal relationships, and have the abilities and talents to tackle whatever they will encounter in life. And when Mom and Dad aren't around, these adolescents can stand tall and strong against the culture to make good choices and healthy decisions.

Sadly many parents today are more concerned about maintaining a friendship with their kids and doing more for their kids than their parents did for them—as if doing things for your kids is a mark of a good parent. If I had a dollar for every time a kid said to me, "I wish my parents would be the parents I need them to be, not the parent that I sometimes want them to be," I'd be a rich man.

Parenting Is Not about Us

When it comes to parenting, it's not about us. It's about our kids. Our parenting should not be a display of effort to try to be recognized as parent of the year, but ours should be lives filled with actions that teach our kids how to develop discernment, moral values, and compassion for the world around them.

Mom and dads, your teens don't need more friends; they need a parent. They need a close relationship with someone who is determined to teach them how to survive in a world where responsibility is an essential character trait.

>>> 4 <<<

No One Gets Respect

er parents named her Kaylee; I nicknamed her "Skunk." The first time I saw Kaylee she was directing her deluge of disrespect toward her parents who silently sat and cried as she pummeled them with accusatory bombshells of contempt, conjuring up anything she could to hurt the two people who had spent a lifetime offering her nothing but a wonderful home filled with love and acceptance. Her parents' comments to me hinted that Kaylee had been a good kid, until she turned thirteen and turned vicious toward them. I eventually nicknamed her "Skunk" because of my first encounter with her when the interaction, described in one word, stunk. Not to mention that she also had a bleached white stripe down the middle of her long, black hair.

The first time we met, I approached her and greeted her. Not knowing that I was the founder of the place where she was going to be spending the next year of her life, she responded by asking in a monotone voice, "What do you do here?" Taking advantage of her ignorance, and wanting to add a bit of levity to the situation, I told her, "I'm the maintenance man." Her cool response was, "Really? Well, you need to do a better job because this place is a dump." With voices bouncing around in my head that shouted, *Respect your elders* and *Make a good first impression*, I realized that my maturity and experience meant nothing to this young lady.

If respect is an outward expression showing a deep admiration toward someone because of their abilities, qualities, or achievements, there was none here. Thus began a relationship between a skunk and a maintenance man.

Skunk was really no different than most kids today. Her parents were loving people, only wanting the best for Skunk, and they had a wonderful relationship with her all through her preteen years. If they faulted at anything, it was that they underestimated the influence of a culture that was exposing their child to way too much way too early (see chapter 1), and how the lack of real connections in her life (see chapter 2) were affecting their connection with their daughter. Her parents were blindsided by the change in her teen years, and Skunk was being influenced without even knowing it.

Like many kids, Skunk was withholding respect for authorities in her life who potentially could be held as a source of wisdom because she was blindsided by the cultural influence.

As parents allow more freedoms to their child as they age, chances are they will be exposed to more information online. As they are introduced on the Internet to new perspectives and alternative ways of life, something changes. They hear more, see more, and experience more as they also begin to feel more, think about life more, their identity, and where they "fit" in society. All happening as their world is expanding beyond their family's influence.

What Captures Their Attention

Think about what a preteen or teen hears, sees, or reads about—not about what captures *our* attention, but what captures *their* attention. And what captures their attention most are those stories and images about people. They watch reality shows, read stories about celebrities, and are attracted by scandals, gossip, real-life interaction, and sexually charged reporting.

There are more videos because there are more video cameras capturing activities. There are more pictures because most people have a camera on their smart phones in their pockets. There are more TV stations to report. There are more radio stations, Internet newscasts, and weather channels to tune into. More sources of news and networks of information let us know quickly of any happening or activity that is taking place.

There is so much information that it's difficult for teens and pre-teens to decipher what has been exaggerated from the cold, hard truth. And on top of it all, much information gets twisted to satisfy the agendas of anyone promoting their cause or supporting their mission. One group tells us one thing; another group tells us another.

The intent here is to talk about that same mechanism in which information about all these happenings and actions is transferred and what that mechanism is doing to teens and how it affects their concept of respect for those in authority.

That *mechanism* is the widespread distribution of information. The *message* is the opinion formed from the delivery of their data. The *target* seems to be those in authority, or those of high stature. And the *result* is the interpretation of the message in the mind and heart of a young person who can barely sift through all the piles of information to determine what is truth and what is falsehood.

I feel like I possess a pretty good level of discernment in scrutinizing what I listen to and what I watch. It comes with the wisdom of age. But I have to admit; even I don't know what to believe many times when I have so much information piled on my sometimes-slow-filtering brain. If at times, I have trouble sifting fact from fiction and what's real from what's an accusatory attack, I can only imagine the difficulty that teens have in their assessment.

So when they hear about a few crooked politicians, do you think they question all politician's intent? When they hear of teachers having sex with fellow students, does it change their concept of teachers? If a child hears about the sexual trysts of one president, do you think it changes their perspective of all that hold that office? What do you think many kids think of priests with all the reported sexual abuse saturating the news? When a child hears of a professional athlete's life failures, does it taint their image of professional athletes? How about when a minister of the gospel is sleeping with another man's wife and they find out about it? Or hearing about a Boy Scout leader who's not leading boys down the right path? Or worse, it's disheartening when they hear of a parent who has killed their own child or spouse or has abandoned their family. I wonder how a teen interprets the excessive and sometimes embellished information spouted over and over on so many news sources.

When the distribution of information turns from happenings and actions to those people in authoritative places, and the intensity of the news output is rapid and constant and often exaggerated, a teen who lacks a developed skill of discernment will either shut off the input, or worse, lose all respect for a person in a position of authority, and consequently loose respect for others in similar positions.

Shifts in Teens' View of Authority

I have a tremendous respect and admiration for people in positions of authority. I have that respect because I have been the recipient of their kindness, gratitude, and service. And I rarely heard anything negative about authority figures while I was growing up—either because it didn't happen, or things just weren't exposed or mentioned. As a result, I didn't lose respect. But that's not the way it is today. Kids and teens today have heard it all, and they do not hold people in authoritative positions in high regard.

I mentioned in an earlier chapter that I feel teens live in a world dominated by judgment of others where the intention of so many is to *discredit* those few in positions of authority, rather than giving the *credit* that is due so many. There are just as many heroes and great acts from deservingly respectful people; young people just don't hear these stories often from the media. One bad apple doesn't always spoil the bushel, but it seems that the "bad apple" is all we hear about. And when that is all that teens hear about, they eliminate apples from their diet.

So most teens don't believe as their parents do about people in authority. Respect is no longer given just because one holds a position. The eroding of trust begins as the deluge of information moves from a trickle that begins early to a turbulent, treacherous river of negativity that lingers long to discredit and eliminate the respect of authority in their life. And the effect is a shifting of their mind-set about respect.

That *first shift* is when teens shift their respect for people to a respect for things and possessions, which further fuels their sense of entitlement. Parents, and others, are viewed as a means to an end rather than a source of knowledge and understanding. It's in this world of appearance and performance that possessions are critical to teens, and anger is the emotional response to not getting what one wants.

The *second shift* of respect is that adolescents often don't give respect unless it is earned. Theirs is a mind-set that simply says to all authority figures, "If you want respect, then you show me respect."

The *third shift* of respect is that many teens expect to see "bad" before they see the "good" in someone. Childish as it may sound, it's an attempt to protect themselves from having to untangle so much information. In many ways, it's easier just to assume that something is bad rather than to integrate new concepts.

And the sad result of this shift is that wisdom is rejected before it ever has a chance to either be displayed with actions or come out of one's mouth. That's what happened to Skunk. She cut off the escape route (her parents, other parents, teachers, coaches, and others she had once respected) from the world of confusion she found herself in, and was then doomed to try to survive in her own world of disconnected relationships.

This shifting of respect and consequential cut-off of the impartation of wisdom from potential respected resources, coupled with lack of relational connections with peers creates an atmosphere that fuels and magnifies normal adolescent attitudes and characteristics and plummets teens deeper in despair.

Normal teenage angst can be described as feelings of dread and anxiety about the human condition, apprehension about one's ability to handle goals and expectations, the feelings of unhappiness, that no one understands them, and they're just angry for no reason. Bad news affirms their perception of a cruel and suffering world, and worry and feeling of uncertainty may overwhelm their attitudes and ability to pull out of their "funk," making the seventh and eighth grades an emotional roller-coaster ride. For many, this is just a normal part of adolescence years that will pass, but for others, this angst elevates to the point of anxiety that takes over one's emotions.

Skunk entered her adolescent years and encountered the

accelerated exposure, the great disconnect from people, the bombardment of information, and the elimination of respected individuals in her life as a cultural wave swept her away to a deserted island of self-sufficiency and self-reliance. Left to her own survival, she began to engage in behaviors hardly acceptable by her parents, and barely right in her own eyes to get her through her turbulent teen years. During this time loving and wise people offered help, but they were only allowed to stand by and watch a tragedy happen.

Respect Begins at Home

Do you think that respect is important? I don't flinch a bit when I tell parents that it is one of the most important attributes that should be displayed in the home, it is the single most important quality that parents can require and facilitate within their home. Disrespect should be met with consequences at any level of your child's development. Equally, respect for each other and in particular those that have something to offer your child, has got to be encouraged and home-grown. There is hope, there is opportunity, and you can keep this wave from destroying a concept of respect that you've developed through the years with your child. Here are some important considerations.

1. Know the wave is coming. Don't be blindsided. Your child will be influenced by the culture's disrespect, and it is better to start having discussion early before your child loses respect, than to wait until your child has already lost it and eliminates you from his or her world.

2. Give your child an example that is worthy of respect. It's difficult to talk about respect if you're not worthy of respect in

the eyes of your child. And if you have made mistakes that have discredited your personal example, just the identifying of that blemish and asking your child for forgiveness has an amazing way of redeeming respect within the family. Don't merely say you're sorry, but also ask for forgiveness. Saying you're sorry sometimes just covers your transgression; asking for forgiveness shouts of wanting to restore a relationship.

3. Discuss with your children what media is saying about celebrities and public authority figures. When you hear of any authority who has fallen, be quick to discuss what has happened to keep the seeds of discord or discredit from rooting in the heart of your child.

4. Talk about people you respect. I'm sure that you've heard that it takes four positive comments to make up for the damage of one negative comment. Same is true here. Let your child know of stories of integrity and courage. Share stories with them about influential people in your life. Let them know that they can't always believe what they hear and say, but they can always rely on your example and your truthfulness. The reason this is so important is that I've found that once there is a lack of respect of relationships within a home, there is usually an overwhelming lack of respect for others and a disregard for the position of authority people hold—in particular, parents.

How's my relationship with Skunk now? It is one of great mutual respect. But it didn't come because I demanded or expected it. It happened because I was intentional about not only building respect into our relationship, but keeping it from being lost.

That's a relationship worthy of respect.

>>> 5 <<<

Loss of Gender Differences

Oddly, as I write this I am on a plane to San Francisco and then on to Toronto to lead parenting seminars, on a day that is officially a coming-out day for those who want to proclaim their sexual bias.

Things were very different when I was growing up. I was born in the west Texas town of Midland, where the land is dry and barren but the people are welcoming and the sunsets are magnificent. We lived in many other little towns as my dad hopscotched across the Texas desert in search of black gold. I remember my first pair of cowboy boots, and a scrapbook filled with old black-and-white Polaroid pictures from the late 1950s confirm my childhood love for guns, holsters, and stick horses.

One of the kids who live on our Heartlight campus recently asked me what TV shows I watched when I was a kid. And as I thought about it, I realized the majority of shows I watched were cowboy shows. They were weekly programs that molded my thinking and gave me a clear picture of what a true man was. They were Westerns like *The Rifleman, Gunsmoke, The Lawman, How the West Was Won, Bonanza, Wagon Train, Rawhide*, and *Have Gun Will Travel*. Should I go on? I also watched *Wyatt Earp, Paladin, Maverick, Laramie*, and *The Virginian*. More? I never missed *The Big Valley, Roy Rogers, The Lone Ranger, Shenandoah*, or *Bat*

Masterson. I had never stopped to think about the influence these shows had on me as I grew up.

I now have a closet full of boots, collect old Western pistols and Winchester rifles, love looking at the stars, enjoy campfires, and own a couple dozen horses. I think it all stems from those old shows I grew up watching. Perhaps that's why I live in the country; sport a mustache that resembles one gracing the face of cowboys from the 1880s; love rodeos, Western movies, and country music; and feel so comfortable around those who work the land and raise cattle and horses. (I still dream of one day riding on a cattle drive.) Denim and Western shirts are my clothing of choice. Why, I even recently read a book on the history of barbed wire in Texas (boring to most, but intriguing to me). But that's not the only way those old Westerns affected me.

The heroes of those Westerns taught me about what it is to be a man. The shows I watched, emulated, and dreamed about imparted concepts on my heart and shaped my thinking to stand up for and do what is right, to fight for what you believe in, to stand firm when truth is on the line, to keep your word, and to treat a woman like a lady. Marshall Dillon and Miss Kitty would be proud.

Those old Westerns formulated my concept of manhood, which is, in many ways, still my definition of who I strive to be today.

How the Media Shapes Our Teens

With that backdrop, I wonder a great deal about what shows teens watch to determine what their concept of who they are and who they are to become. I mull over what young girls today observe that determines their concept of what it is to be a woman . . . and agonize over what young boys see that provides that imagery of what it is to be a man.

The concept of social gender is quite different than it was during the age of those old Westerns. It's just not as clear as it used to be. Most men on television today are portrayed as buffoons, idiots, silly, stupid, violent, or abusive where the display of masculinity has become politically incorrect—far from the images of manliness portrayed years ago. On those same programs, women are often depicted as intellectually superior, sassy, and way too sexual for comfort for this cowboy. And this portrayal of men and women in today's media causes confusion about the roles of men and women in society.

Years ago, I watched a little girl named Chastity, the daughter of Sonny and Cher, being introduced to the world on her parents' variety show. In 2011, I watched this Chastity, who is now Chaz, perform on the TV show *Dancing with the Stars*, not as a woman but as a transformed man. I hear songs on the radio where girls are kissing girls and they like it. I see two guys getting married, and a woman exchanging marriage vows with another woman on the courthouse steps as judiciary magistrates try to determine the far-reaching implications of equality among sexes. Many feel the definition of marriage between a man and woman is not socially encompassing as it currently is. And tolerance and acceptance of sexuality as defined however anyone wants it to be is commonplace.

Adolescent guys are rarely taught through today's media how to become strong, capable, loving, faithful men. I think it's important for them to learn that they can be gentle without being gay. They can be strong without being violent. And they can care about girls without being "pimps." Many don't know how to be men of integrity, so instead they talk big, think appearance is everything, and act their manhood out sexually when it should be an expression of their heart. Confusing for young men? You bet.

I recently asked a young man on our *Parenting Today's Teens* radio program what it meant to be a man. He replied, "It's confusing to me." He went on to explain that, after watching his father, he thought that being a man meant you had to make a lot of money and provide for your family. After watching other young men around him, he thought he had to be a tough guy, always challenging, judging, and overpowering his peers with bravado and swagger. The message he said he got from his youth minister was that a man had to be tender and caring. Girls he talked to said a man had to be attractive, have expensive things, and be sexual in his approach to girls. Of course he's a little confused—who wouldn't be without examples of true manliness being displayed and the concept of manhood being redefined in social and media circles?

Girls are just as confused and conflicted. On one hand they are told they need to be dainty and always in need of being rescued, but on the other hand they are told they are just as capable as any male. Young girls begin to believe, at the urging of male peers, that they must send nude pictures of themselves to boys to show their wares, yet they are chastised for going too far. And girls who long to connect with peers are encouraged to prove their womanhood by acting out sexual rituals, instead of demonstrating the character qualities they possess.

On a recent trip to Starbucks with a group of girls from our Heartlight campus, I was asked a question that revealed their confusion about sexuality and gender differences. This is a group I had spent quite a bit of time teaching how to ride horses, so I knew the girls and genuinely believe they were searching more than they were shocking me by their question. One girl asked, "Mark, if you came home from work and found your wife in bed with someone, would you rather have it be a man or a woman?" Needless to say, my jaw dropped and I don't know whether I was more dumb-founded by the question, my inability to give an answer, or by the intensity of her curiosity. Her question and true search for an answer revealed her confusion about sexuality and the complexity of searching for the truth in a social arena that she knew was say-ing otherwise.

My point is not to debate the issues of homosexuality or equal opportunity among the sexes. My position is merely to say that amid all the difficulties that kids are facing today, the loss of gen-der differences is just one more complication that presents itself to teens. The issue of "what is a man?" or "what is a woman?" is not as clear-cut as it used to be, and parents must address this confusion unless moms and dads want society to dictate those def-initions for their children. One of the parent's roles in the life of a child is to give clarity, discussion, and explanation to gender issues.

I'm all for women having the same opportunities as men (women now outnumber men in the US workforce).[1] I believe no one should be restrained from opportunity or being given a chance solely because of gender. I don't believe anyone should be discrimi-nated against or held back from positions in the workplace that they are more than capable to fill. But I do believe that there are differences between a man and a woman. And I further believe that many of those valuable differences become lost in the attempt to equalize changing gender roles in society.

And this becomes difficult for parents when parents feel like their child's role should follow one direction, and the child, in a search for his or her own identity, doesn't agree with what a parent wants. Here's an example.

I recently met with a group of mothers (150 of them) and asked them what the role of a wife is in the home. Many stated that they believe that a wife should be virtuous, respect her husband, take care of the kids, prepare healthy food for her family, be wise in spending money, and not grumble while doing tasks. These are among the characteristics listed in Proverbs 31, a Bible passage that is often quoted and taught in churches. When I mentioned these characteristics to a group of teenage girls, the girls unanimously voiced strong disagreements with this role of a woman in a marriage. One of the girls said, "This is why I think the church and its teachings are so outdated and don't apply to my world."

Cultural Influences about Gender Roles

This culture influences our children greatly. The conversation about the definition of marriage is a huge debate that, if it hasn't already, will cause quite a bit of conversation among teens. And the gay rights issue isn't going to go away anytime soon. There isn't a day that goes by that I don't hear of families struggling with the confusion surrounding girl-girl relationships, gay friendships, and alternative lifestyles.

Just this morning, I received an e-mail from a mom who was desperate to know what to do with her daughter. Her well-behaved, modest sweetheart took a picture of herself kissing another girl and texted it to a few of her friends—only to have the picture go viral and land in the hands of the principal, who promptly expelled both girls for "inappropriate behavior."

A few weeks ago, a father called bewildered about what to do with his son, who took a manly position to defend the honor of his sister who was called a "slut" by some peers, and after being physically pushed, he punched the aggressor, unintentionally breaking his nose. Charges were filed, the son was expelled from school, and the dad was lost about how to respond to his son's statement: "Dad, I was fighting for the dignity of my sister. I was defending her. I was protecting her. Didn't you say that girls are a beauty to fight for? You've told me to always stand up and be a man . . . Why am I being punished for that?"

Needless to say confusion surrounds the definition of appropriateness and the understanding of gender roles in the teen culture. One would have to argue with me for a long, long time to convince me otherwise of these two things.

First, inside the heart of every teen girl is the longing to be valued for who she is and not what she can do sexually. And second, inside the heart of every teen guy is a desire to express his manhood through something more than the size of his body parts, what toys he owns, or how he performs physically or academically. Every woman wants a prince, every kid wants a hero, and every man wants to be both.

I'm equally convinced of this: how these kids are to achieve this longing is a confusing and bewildering process as they interpret the messages from the culture they inhabit. And that confusion is worsened when their parents' actions at home reveal the parents are somewhat confused about what a true man or a true woman looks like.

Moms, physical appearance is a part of being a woman. But you need to teach your daughter that true beauty is a condition of the heart that is shown through love and fervor for life and people.

Men and others will be drawn to the inner beauty of compassion, kindness, and wisdom.

And dads, manliness isn't displayed by your ability to ride a Harley, kill wild animals, bend steel in your bare hands, ride a bucking bronco, play sports well, drive a nice car, or own a large house. True manliness has more to do with virility, courage, bravery, and being comfortable in your own skin.

I believe that gender roles have more to do with *who* you are and the ideals you embrace than what you have, do, or display. As parents and children alike focus on developing an inner strength and beauty as conditions of our hearts, we'll discover that the character traits we embrace will stand out as examples to our culture of true manliness and real womanhood.

>>> 6 <<<

Living with Constant Uncertainty

You can be certain that your kids will one day realize the uncertainty of life. When I think about what kids view and hear today, it's no surprise that many kids entering adolescence are filled with questions, undecided about which paths to take, not sure they're ready to face the world, and uncertain whether what they've been taught will help them in the future. They live with constant uncertainty. The doubt, hesitation, and indecision that is common to adolescence has been further confused and complicated by a time that shouts boldly the messages of doom and gloom that intensify their uncertainty, pushing ordinary adolescent angst to teen anguish, and normal hesitancy to higher levels of unhealthy anxiety. And the pushback is great.

They hear rumors that the end of the world is coming soon. They witness the loss of life by natural disasters that sweep across distant shores killing hundreds of thousands or rattle islands that crumbled with a death toll too unimaginable to comprehend. They hear of war and rumors of war, and watch movies at the local theater about the earth's demise. They live in a time of economic crisis and hear the outspoken critics of the gloom of the world. They see the broken promises for jobs and positions to those who complete their education. Our government is out of money, Wall Street's volatility screams "uncertainty," terrorism is a constant threat, businesses are failing, and nothing feels secure.

The bombardment of information captures teens' hearts and teases their imagination, leading them to think that all is worse than it actually is. They read more about the deaths from cancer than they do the progress of finding a cure, and they hear more about teen suicide than ever before.

I'm not naive to think that I grew up in a world where there weren't any problems. Vietnam, the assassination of a president and a civil rights leader, hurricanes that battered the coast, riots in the streets, the Kent State shootings, a tornado that destroyed my home, and the 1972 Olympics in Munich all showcased the uncertainty of life. But I never quit believing that if I just did things right, kept my nose clean, and worked hard, that I would be successful. Any ten-year period since then has been filled with some uncertainty and calamity. Uncertainty by itself is not that much different from the uncertainty we've all experienced. But today, uncertainty is magnified by the exposure given and interpreted with deeper intensity than it was even a few years ago. And its reach has touched the lives of the once protected and innocent lives of tweens and preteens.

The Cycle of Uncertainty

Today's teenagers experience a lack of connection with peers and adults. They are irresponsible because of parental involvement that borders on hovering and even codependency. Lack of respect for authority flourishes. And confusion about gender differences adds to the puzzlement of the times. These ingredients of confusion all funnel into one arena at a time in a teenager's life when the natural consequences for missteps, poor choices, indecisive action, and curiosity can be of great magnitude. That arena is one of uncertainty. The earlier they experience the realization of this, the earlier problems with its acceptance are shown.

Kids become uncertain about what they've been taught, what they believe, who their friends are, how they are supposed to act, what's going to last, and how they should perform. They begin to wonder if the embraced values and principles that Mom and Dad have taught them really work. They question what they believe. They wonder if they really are who they have been led to believe they are. Some are unprepared to handle the overload of information they begin to receive, unaware of their own immaturity, irresponsibility, and inabilities.

Little princesses are coming home with broken tiaras wondering if they really are the royalty their parents always said they were. Young men begin to realize their physical and mental limitations. They come home often feeling like losers when all they've been taught is that they're winners. Young girls face their sexuality early when many of their peers begin their menstrual cycles. And young men are exposed to explicit images of women through easy access to pornographic material.

During adolescence, kids begin to find out that certain heroes aren't quite the heroes they thought they were. Their accessibility to the Internet to search for answers begins to create less of a dependence on Mom and Dad at a time when they need them the most. They begin to question the goodness of life when they experience rejection, ridicule, and the cruelty of peers. The inclusiveness of their elementary school years trickles to exclusiveness. Social selection has begun.

So they come home and vent their frustration by yelling at

parents or siblings, kicking the dog, or retreating to their room to process the day's activities. They may withdraw and become more silent. Many become engrossed in video games and activities that help them rest, find comfort, or avoid the thoughts racing through their heads. Their tears express their feelings of frustration; their moodiness exemplifies their emotional turmoil. They are overwhelmed. There's a lot to process.

The junior high years usher in a whole new world of opportunity. It's a phase of exploring curiosities and testing the limits with experimentation. It's a time that teens look for a connection in fulfilling their longing for belonging. They experience more rejection in activities and social circles, which fuels their discussions and accusations toward one another. Social networks such as Facebook become an obsession. Cyberbullying transforms little princesses to drama queens. And young men become tough guys wrangling for social position, fueled by raging hormones and false images of the opposite sex. Texting is the preferred mode of communication, and appearance is the source of value for kids who begin to feel a sense of loss. Some young men begin to toy with thoughts that because of their rejection from the opposite sex and their lack of fulfilling opposite sex relationships, they might just be gay and want to try that lifestyle. Many values that were once certain move to the uncertain column.

Many teens from faith-based homes enter their adolescent years eager to keep themselves pure, clean, abstinent, drug-free, safe, and committed to their faith. Then the battle begins, and they discover that the cultural pressure is far stronger than they thought. Hesitantly, one girl kisses another to see if there's any truth to this girl-girl relationship thing. Guys might grab a beer or smoke pot for the first time. Alcohol might be consumed to see what it's like while spending the night at a friend's. Movies are watched at friends' homes where parents allow more than what is allowed at home. The exposure continues, and the experimentation begins. Many teens find excitement in new activities when older activities have become boring. And some find that the new pursuits help them make new connections in hopes of filling voids caused by unrewarding relationships.

Senior high kids learn through their experimental trysts that they'll either stay where they are in regard to values, principles, and biblical standards, or they will embrace the mentality of "if you can't beat 'em, join 'em." Many times I've listened to parents who tell me that their son went upstairs to bed being one person they knew completely and came downstairs the next day a complete stranger. It's a change that seems to happen in the blink of an eye. The confidence felt during the junior high years is replaced by confusion and embarrassment in the senior high years. And most kids, feeling judged and shameful, disconnect from the world that taught them the values they believe in and embrace the world that offers a temporary reprieve from the confusion they feel.

Looking for Something New and Exciting

Megan is a young lady who, at age fifteen, said that she got bored and wanted something new and exciting. Her involvement in school and church was stellar, she had worked as a summer camp counselor, and her parents' role in her life was engaging. She shared with me how she was one person at home and another at school. Eventually, tired of the pressure she felt from both settings, she defaulted to the one where she spent the most time and was the least conflictive. The world of sexual promiscuity and alcohol became a place of escape for her.

Eric, a fifteen-year-old, told me that when he smoked pot for the first time, he felt as though all the pressures he was feeling in junior high were lifted from him. He said that retreat was a better option than always engaging in battle. Sadly, he shared how the judgment of his well-meaning friends only caused him to embrace the world of drugs. He said that he felt normal when he smoked, more loved with his new friends than all his good friends, and more encouraged than criticized by the people in his new life.

Your confident and convinced kids will come to that fork in the road where they will make decisions about what they want, choose the path that they think will get them there, and settle into the journey that is usually the path of least resistance and helps them temporarily remove confusion and engage in short-term relationships.

This indecisiveness thrives in a world of constant uncertainty that calls into question which course to follow. In the teenage years, kids are caught in a cultural whirlpool that feels welcoming, attractive, and intriguing—even though it runs counter to their beliefs. They twirl and whirl and often give up, knowing they should reach out their hand for the life preserver their parents are holding but are unable or unwilling to muster the strength to grab it.

It's happening. And we can't ignore the impact this is having on our families and the effect it's having on our kids.

Many teenagers experience the uncertainty of life when the actions of others challenge the confidence of a gentle heart longing for security amidst an unsure world. That experience may be encountered when a child hears that Mom and Dad will no longer be married or a tragedy changes the course of a child's existence, both conveying the message that what was once counted on, can no longer be. The experience might be couched in a divorce, a death, or a disease that alters the plans and dreams of a lifetime.

Or it may just be, that as a child ages, that they become aware of the condition of the world and without anything to compare their thinking to, adopt a resolution to make sure that the disappointment of uncertainty can be overcome with thoughts of resolve to make things certain and attainable.

Two Responses to Uncertainty

I've seen kids respond to uncertainty in one of two ways. The first response is one when a child thinks, *Okay, if everything is so uncertain, then I'm going to take control and make sure there's some things that are certain in my life.* They determine to control their own destiny. They tank their once embraced values and principles developed in an atmosphere of certainty, and grab hold of new values that promise results and answers in a world of uncertainty. They make goals and commit to fulfill their need to know that their efforts will not come back void.

The second response to uncertainty is just to give up and live a life that is entirely opposite of the first response. They choose to spin out of control recklessly, not thinking about consequences of life choices. Their mentality is rooted in behavior that expresses the frivolousness of a life where certainty doesn't exist. Their motto might be, "Whatever I do doesn't matter, anyway." Skepticism invades a once certain world where a young heart, disappointed by an equation for life that doesn't add up, becomes diseased by the absence of trust, care, or engaging feelings.

It's a different world today than it was just a few years ago. And as it speeds up and exposes us all to more and more, the world's influence calls parents to fill with certainty the voids caused in a child's life as they experience uncertainty. Parents can't always change the influence of the world, but they can change the way they engage with their kids to help them weather the storms of uncertainty.

Moms and Dads, the new influences of today's teen culture need to be battled with a new model of parenting. Commit yourself to shaking off some old, ineffective ways of parenting and embrace some of these new concepts that will offer your kids hope and help through their adolescent years.

It'll give your kids something to be certain about.

>>> **Part Two** <<<

Parenting
Practices to Avoid

>>> 7 <<<

Perfection Is Impossible

Newly married, I took a job at a church because the pastor was excited about the work I had done with Young Life and he thought I could bring some of that excitement from a parachurch organization to a church youth group. It was the beginning of a wonderful time with kids, and the start of a seven-year journey working for a man who demanded perfection in everything, perfection moved us to offering programs, relationships, and a helping hand to literally thousands of kids throughout the city of Tulsa, Oklahoma. He would always say, "Matthew 5:48, Matthew 5:48" ("Be perfect, therefore, as your heavenly Father is perfect" NIV). He was a man I loved, admired, and who spoke a lot about grace. But he wore out his staff with a mind-set that was, I believe, rooted in wanting a spirit of excellence but was interpreted by the church staff as a demand to be perfect in all we do.

That mind-set drove me. I worked seven days a week, felt guilty when I wasn't working, never took a vacation, couldn't rest, could barely sleep, always had to look good and have it all together, and constantly felt that there was always more to do and never enough hours in the day to get it done. I felt like the only time the senior pastor enjoyed my presence was when I was telling him how everything was bigger and better, how we had no conflicts in the youth group, how great he was, and how perfect everyone in my charge was doing. (I lied to him many times.) And you know what? We were successful in creating some pretty neat programs and activities for junior and senior high students. With a few hundred kids in the youth group, Bible studies galore, many small groups, and mission trips every summer, our youth ministry was doing well. All under the banner of "perfection." It almost cost me my marriage.

Overwhelmed by the Demand for Perfection

The other ministers in charge of different areas of ministry expressed that they felt the same way. Five of us would gather once a week for breakfast just to talk about life and work, encourage one another, and we became good friends with one thing in common: our marriages were struggling. All were great guys, good friends, competent performers, and highly driven. It was tough. And we all thought we were doing the right thing by trying to live up to this concept of perfection. In reality, we were all burning out and didn't know it. My wake-up call was when my daughter didn't even recognize me when I picked her up from day care. Deep down, I was miserable. I didn't want to slow down because I'd have to think about the path I was on, and I didn't feel like I could question my so-called perfect life. My dream of perfection was fading.

One of the guys on our staff decided to leave his position because his marriage was falling apart. His departure was hard on me as he was someone I felt was a good friend, a trusted peer, a great communicator full of wisdom and discernment, and seemed to have it all together. When he left, there wasn't any ceremony (sadly) acknowledging his years of service, so I took him out to eat to express my appreciation for his friendship. When I asked him what he'd like to say to the church if he were given an opportunity, he said, "Tell the senior pastor that he's not God."

Remember the old 1960s song "I Gotta Get Out of This Place" by Eric Burdon and the Animals? I hummed it driving all the way back to the church and started that day planning my exit strategy from perfectionism. Once I left, I never again saw or talked to that senior pastor. If he only knew the damage he caused in so many of the lives of people who had worked for him. This kind man didn't know, just like so many parents today who are clueless about the messages they send to their kids through actions, comments, requirements, and lifestyles.

Perfection was impossible back then. Perfection is impossible now. The difference now is that the damage is greater because of the shift in the youth culture, thus causing kids to interpret parents' encouragement, holding to morals and biblical principles, and sharing of wisdom as being critical.

The Chipping Away of "Perfection"

Remember when your kids were young and you could do no wrong? Your kids thought then that you were perfect. You coached their teams, told them they were all winners, and scheduled your life around them. You laughed with them, hauling them to all their activities, and scheduled your days around your kids. You poured your life into them. And chances are, you believed that if you did these things with your kids, then everything would turn out well in their teen years—an investment during the early years brings reward in future years. Right? Unfortunately, it doesn't always work that way.

Here's what I think happens. During those early years, kids think their parents are perfect. They don't see the flaws, the blemishes, and the pimples of life. You protect them, provide for them, and aim to please them—nothing wrong with those actions. But in their mind, they think you are perfect. Young girls and boys usually think that about their parents.

So these little princes and princesses enter their middle school years, believing they live in a perfect world and have perfect parents. They soon find out that the world isn't so perfect. They begin to learn that the world is cruel, comments are harsh, people are mean, and not everyone is good. They're exposed to more, experience more, and encounter more than they ever thought and perhaps beyond what they were trained to handle. In their attempt to make sense of the world and apply what they have learned their whole life, they come home emotionally spent and then interpret their parents' well-intended comments of encouragement and direction as a demand for perfection.

Here's what's shifted. All during their younger years, you've added to your children's life. Now you're helping them rid themselves of unhealthy and inappropriate actions and mind-sets that enter their, and your, world. It's like that old adage, "You spend the first two years of your child's life teaching them to talk and walk, and the rest of their life telling them to shut up and sit down." The author of the book *The Little Prince*, Antoine de Saint-Exupery, is reported to have said, "Perfection is finally attained not when there is no longer anything to add but when there is no longer anything to take away." This quote reminds me of the actions of many parents. Spending the first years of their child's life "adding" to it, they spend the teen years "taking away" any influences counter to what was added. It's this chipping away that moves kids to think their parents want perfection, are nagging all the time, and are never satisfied with them. Sadly, many parents spend their child's preteen years telling them what they're doing right and their teen years telling them what they're doing wrong. The good intention of parents is sometimes interpreted as a negative action by their kids.

Adolescents interpret their parents' encouragement as judgment. Parents' standards are interpreted as too high of expectations. Questions are interpreted as digging for more dirt. Discussions are interpreted as inquiries into privacy. Compliments are interpreted as being critical. And a desire for a spirit of excellence is interpreted as a quest for perfection.

Parents feel they can't win, no matter what they do.

Here's the good news. You're not God. And you're not perfect either. It may be time to break the "perfect" image your kids have of you. Parents who don't break the perfection mentality with their kids might just hear their kids saying what a group of kids said to me last week when I asked them, "Do you think your parents want perfection in you?" Here are their answers:

- "I brought home some grades I was proud of and my mom started complaining that I could do better, I wasn't living up to my potential, and I needed to work harder."
- "I never understood how my imperfect parents always demand perfection of me."
- I wish my parents knew that the messiness of my room was just a picture of the messiness I felt in my life. They seem more concerned about my room."

- "I remember when my parents and I had a fight over me not wanting to go to church, and they were so concerned about what others would think if I didn't show up and if we had an argument."
- "I couldn't measure up to my parents' ideal world, so I gave up."
- "I think my rebellion at home was my attempt to prove to them that they don't live in a perfect little world."
- "It's funny to me that we had the most screwed-up family in our whole neighborhood, and our yard was prettier than everyone else's. I think it was my parents' way of pretending to others that we had it all together."
- "I can't wait to leave home so I can relax and enjoy life."
- "I've considered committing suicide, and my parents are more concerned about the cleanliness of my bathroom than the condition of my heart."
- "Sadly, I set out to prove that my life of imperfection was better than their life of perfection."
- "I was sent away to get help for my emotional problems . . . No one in my extended family knows because my parents are scared they won't be seen as good parents if someone knew their child is messed up."
- "I thought my dad hated me because of the zits on my face. He always seemed embarrassed when I showed up around his friends, and he would make excuses to them, in front of me, as to why my face looked so bad. I remember scrubbing so hard that I would cry and wonder what was wrong with me."
- "I got tired of trying to attain something that I could never reach, so I quit trying."

- "My world of conflict with them was easier for me than living up to their world of perfection."
- "I was never good enough in my mother's eyes, so she nagged me all the time to do everything better. I rebelled and acted out just to prove her wrong and to show her that I was in control of my life."
- "Every time I saw my mom's mouth open, I shut my ears to her comments about how I was always failing at something. I think she meant well, but all I heard was, 'You're not good enough,' which is exactly what I was hearing from others every day at school."

Most parents who express a perfectionist mind-set to their kids don't realize it. It's like a cancer you don't realize you have until the symptoms are beyond treatment. But there is treatment for perfectionistic parenting. It's learning how to approach the symptoms in a way that diffuses the powder keg of perfection so that it doesn't damage your kids and make them move away from you relationally.

The message of perfection fuels the attitude that appearance and performance are the priority for relationships with others. It teaches kids that acceptance, love, and engagement with others are based on what you do rather than who you are. Remember, what your kids actually learn from you is based on how your teens perceive you, not on what your intentions are.

What do you think you are teaching your child when you can't settle for anything less than perfect for yourself or your child? You are telling your children that no matter what they do, they'll always be a disappointment; and your children will learn that they will never be good enough to have a relationship with you. This is far different from the mind-set they had about you in their preteen years, isn't it?

The Benefits of Imperfection

A man came up to me during one of my parenting seminars and told me what it was like to be raised in a "perfect" home. His dad was a perfect guy: president of the school board, head of the elder board at church, community "man of the year," successful businessman, recognized by all, and, to everyone who knew him, the epitome of perfection. Then his dad had an affair with the church secretary and everything changed. My response was, "Man, that must have been hard." He said, "No, it gave me hope."

When parents help their kids understand that Mom and Dad aren't perfect and engage with their kids so that messages of encouragement aren't interpreted as a demand for perfection, a number of things happen.

You give your kids permission not to be perfect and to feel comfortable in their own skin as they enter their teen years. They begin to look at you, their parent, as one who might just possess wisdom amid imperfection and feel a connection of relationship that validates them by who they are, not by what they do or how they look. It lets them know that they won't be perfect this side of heaven. It might just turn their hearts toward the One who wants to fill the voids and losses in their life. And this parenting mind-set of grace and forgiveness lets teens know it's okay not to have it all together and gives them permission to struggle well during their time of moving from childhood to adolescence.

>>> 8 <<<

Authority Cannot Be Forced

When I started working with teens more than three decades ago, on occasion, I would have to confront inappropriate behaviors with kids I didn't even know. In those days, a stern discussion, a verbal reprimand, or a threat of eliminating a person from group activities if the inappropriate behavior continued was all it took to solve the problem. My remedies to these little challenges worked because most kids had a basic respect of authority and would take correction. So kids made changes in their behavior mainly because of my authority and because they respected me.

As I began working with kids who displayed harder-to-deal-with behaviors, I ramped up what I thought would be effective to get a child to stop the inappropriate behavior and engage in a positive behavior. I used those skills I had grown to know: be strong, administer punishment that caught their attention, and enforce their submission verbally or aggressively, kind of like a drill sergeant. At that time, kids would make changes based on a healthy fear instilled in them by either their parents or other authorities.

These kids feared the consequences of getting spanked, a pop on the knuckles at the dinner table, or a ruler to the hand in a classroom. My dad's discipline of choice was a belt. Discipline techniques of old would have the parents' accompanying sayings of "I brought you into this world, and I can take you out," and "I don't care what other parents let their kids do," "I'm going to knock you clean into next week," and "I'll give you something to cry about." And many times all it took was an "I'm disappointed in you" from a stern-faced dad to bring a misbehaving child to tears and let him know that the behavior must stop.

Even schoolteachers exercised their authority by taking misbehaving kids in the hallways of public schools and giving swats. Coaches would have disrespectful students "grab their ankles." Parents would discipline their disobedient children in public. Even I became accustomed to getting a spanking at five o'clock when my dad got home from work, should I have had the misfortune of wrongdoing that day. A pretty physical display of authority, wasn't it?

Parenting techniques that worked in one generation don't necessarily work in another generation. What I hear from kids of this generation who have been disciplined this way is that they walked away from this type of exercise of authority with a mixture of resentment, humiliation, and a longing for revenge. They speak of now having contempt for authority with an overwhelming sense of helplessness that could only be combated or defended with a strong response, be it verbal or physical. Some might call it rebellion.

Kids don't fear much these days and rarely respect authority. So these antiquated techniques of discipline just don't quite have the impact they used to have and might even be met with defiant responses like, "You do and I'll call child protective services," "I'll call the police," "Just try it!" "You don't scare me," or "You hit me and I'll hit you back," "I don't care."

The discipline techniques of old just don't work like they used to, do they? This isn't a debate on whether you should spank your preteens or paddle your adolescents, or whether there's merit in either. The issue here is that what once worked in parenting no longer works. Authority can't be forced.

Parenting Styles That Backfire

I'm convinced that authority can no longer be forced. The appeal of relationship with your child and winning the right to be heard from your child is sometimes a more effective disciplinary approach, when coupled with other principles I outline in this book. I do believe in rules, consequences, boundaries, high standards, and discipline that helps kids get to a place that they want to be and keeps them from ending up where they don't want to go. But my suggestion is that this happens best when it is cushioned on a foundation of relationship's appeal rather than a show of authority through antiquated means that only damage relationships.

Many parents, when confronted with inappropriate behavior with a child, don't shift their parenting style to create an arena of relationships. Instead, they downshift into a gear that is two steps back and exert their authority; their power, their right, their influence to throw their weight and tout their clout with the intent of "When all else fails, show them who's boss."

Many grandparents feel that if their sons or daughters would just parent differently and spank their kids a little more, their children wouldn't have the problems they're having. They cheer when someone says, "Kids today just need to be raised with a Bible and a belt," and mumble to each other, "It worked for our kids; it should work for them."

Many parents who were disciplined strongly like I was think,

If it was good enough for me, then it's good enough for my kids, so they proceed down this parenting path expecting the same results. But it doesn't happen that way—not because parents don't have the right or because the expression of authority is no longer valid, but because kids today respond differently to authority because of the cultural influence.

Your teenagers are getting beat up verbally at school every day, hearing more and more about the abuse of power by those in authority, and experiencing a time that relationships with friends are weaning. It's a time of change for them and they are becoming independent, thinking through all you have taught them, and trying to apply the principles you have instilled in them. And it is tough. And because it is tough, conflict will happen. When it does happen and you decide to pull out your "authority card" and lay it on the table, you just might not get what you're hoping for.

Here are some ineffective statements I've heard parents say with the intent of showing their authority. They usually backfire and just cause greater problems:

- "It's my way or the highway."
- "You do so because I said so."
- "Do as I say, not as I do."
- "As long as you live in this house, it will be done this way."
- "I don't care what you think; this is our home."
- "You will respect me . . . I'm your father!"
- "You will call your stepmother 'Mom.'"
- "I'll say what I want when I want to say it, and you'll listen or be grounded."
- "I will read and look at anything written in this house."
- "Change your attitude right now!"

- "I don't have to give you a reason."
- "It's my TV, and we will watch what I want to watch."
- "Go to your room now, and don't come back here until you say you're sorry."
- "You will go to church and you will like it."
- "You're a [whatever your last name is], so act like it."
- "Quit crying, you sissy."
- "Here are the things you need to change about yourself . . . and you need to change them now."
- "Here are the things I don't like about you."
- "I don't care whether you think I need to change . . . I'm the parent here."
- "I'm the king of this house and you will do as I say."

Some parents tell me they usually resort to showing their authority when nothing else is working. They tell me that their child doesn't respect them, doesn't submit to their authority, and shows no regard for them as a parent. In response to these parents, I suggest some introspection to see if they're doing anything wrong. There's only one person in the world you can really change, and that's yourself. So look to yourself first, and see if there is any hurtful way in you. Ask the Lord to examine your heart and then lead you in a way that moves the relationship forward. You can't always see the heart of your child, but you can examine your heart to see if there may be some things that need to change and some valid reasons that you're getting some pushback from your kids.

Below is a list of things I see many parents doing that provoke their kids to anger or shut their kids down to any recognition of their authority. Look and see if you display any of these actions toward your kids—or better yet, ask your kids if they see any of these characteristics in you. You might just be undermining your own authority. The purpose here is not to give your kids the opportunity to tear you apart or make you their convenient doormat, but to offer them the opportunity to start a conversation that will improve your relationship with them.

- Setting unrealistic expectations for your child's age
- Neglecting their feelings or comments
- Comparing siblings
- Not listening to their heart
- Embarrassing and ridiculing them
- Not respecting their opinion
- Showing favoritism toward one child over another
- Impatience and frustration accompanied by yelling and screaming
- Insensitivity and unwillingness to validate their feelings
- Sarcasm and name-calling
- Having too many rules and not enough relationship
- Correcting continually where your child doesn't want to be in your presence
- Being preoccupied or too busy with work or others
- Not respecting privacy and their need to have some downtime
- Having too high expectations
- Falsely accusing based on presumption rather than fact
- Always having to be right; can never be wrong
- Pretending to be perfect when they know otherwise
- Lying to your child or misleading them
- Breaking promises
- Overreacting instead of responding

- Overprotecting instead of preparing them for life
- Not respecting child's decisions and shaming them for mistakes
- Not respecting their desires, hopes, and feelings
- Having low expectations of child's ability to think and solve own problems
- Disciplining the child in front of others
- Showing marriage conflict in the extreme
- Making a child take sides between two parents
- Inconsistency of discipline, disagreement between parents in approach
- Never trusting the child
- Inflexibility in what you believe
- Interrupting in conversations
- Being judgmental about friends, decisions, and likes and dislikes
- Telling them how they should feel
- Ridiculing their faults and mistakes
- Always telling them what they need to do
- Expecting unreasonable tasks beyond child's ability
- Being critical in spirit and arrogant in confrontation
- Showing conditional love
- Not explaining why some decisions are made
- Demanding perfection and never being satisfied
- Jumping to conclusions with misuse of your imagination

Change what you can change about yourself as a parent so your kids can learn about your authority through the way you engage with them. Don't force them to have to choose to follow your authority; instead, lead them to an understanding of your authority through the healthy, loving relationship you establish with them.

If you find yourself having to remind people of your authority, you've already lost it. If you discover that you remind people where your authority came from, then you don't carry any with them. And if you catch yourself having to display your authority through any of the prior-mentioned comments or harsh actions, it's time to develop a new parenting strategy.

I know that kids want to show they are mature, in control, and independent, which are all characteristics parents want to be displayed in their children's lives. And I know just as well that kids are more immature than they have ever been with a desire to act more grown up than ever. Your display of old-school authority may just cause them to dig in their heels to prove their maturity, control, and independence. I've seen it with hundreds of kids, and I experience it daily with my pet donkey named Toy.

Playing the "Relationship Card"

Toy is a stubborn donkey. I can try to get her to do something, such as follow me, to listen to instructions, and to avoid something dangerous, but she has a mind of her own and often displays her obstinate nature. So when all my efforts to get her to respond to me aren't working, I find myself wanting to prove my authority by hitting her, pushing her, and yanking on her lead rope until I am worn out. What I have learned is that Toy doesn't respond to authority very well, and my attempts to enforce my authority only hurt our relationship. She digs in her heels, and when it comes to a fight, she won't budge.

Sound familiar? Hey, if you ever feel like you're in a great position of authority, come try to tell Toy what to do; she'll put you in your place quickly.

Here's what I've further learned in my interactions with Toy. If I can get her to think that she wants to do something, and I spend some time enticing, entreating, and encouraging her positively, she'll allow me to walk beside her and all I have to then do is guide her on her path. See the connection I'm making here?

I play the "relationship card" with the teens who live on our Heartlight campus all the time. I'll say, "I'm not asking you to go this way because I'm your authority. I'm asking you to go this way because I want good things for you. I want you to end up in a place where you want to be, not where you don't want to be." I still have the "authority card" in my hand, but I choose to play the "relationship card" because it trumps everything on the table. My authority is shown on the face of that relationship card by the wisdom I bring, the opportunities I provide, the decisions I help them make, and the boundaries I set for them. It's an authority that is won, not demanded; and it is offered, not forced.

People change because of relationship, not authority.

9

Judging Builds Walls

When I was in high school, I loved dogs and critters and wanted to be a veterinarian. I thought this choice of profession would accommodate my love of animals and fulfill my desire to help the underdog. As it turned out, I've spent my life helping "underdogs," but not as a vet. That doesn't mean my love for animals has lessened. I now have the opportunity to do what I wanted to do while helping others. So outside my back door live sixty teenagers: the focus of my profession of helping underdogs. And in my backyard live my dog, my cat, four llamas, one donkey, twenty-four horses, and a host of birds, squirrels, foxes, coyotes, and deer that find sanctuary and safety in our yard also.

Our llamas have always been one of my special projects. These weird-looking animals, which look like a combination of goat, camel, sheep, dog, giraffe, and fur ball all wrapped up into one, have become very dear to me despite the ridicule of many. Our first llamas were named Llama-Llama Ding-Dong, Osama Bin Llama, Yo-Mama-Llama, and Tony Llama (after the famous boot maker). Tony is the focus of this story.

A Judgment Call

One brisk winter morning I got a call from a lady named Cindy who identified herself as sitting in a white car next to the highway that runs next to our property. She proceeded to tell me that one of our horses was lying on the ground in our pasture and needed help. I thanked her for letting me know of the situation and assured her I would get out there quickly and check it out. But she kept informing me of all the things I was doing wrong in the care of our animals (I didn't even know who this lady was).

She stated that she noticed that one of our horses had died a month earlier (as if I didn't know) and hadn't been buried for three days. And she said we should take better care of our animals—adding that if she hadn't called, then we would not know about this struggling horse. She also said that she was going to call the Society for Prevention of Cruelty to Animals (SPCA) to report our abuse and that she should call the sheriff to come take all our animals because I was doing a terrible job in caring for our pets.

At that moment, all I wanted to do was to get out to the field and find the horse that was in trouble. I felt it really wasn't the time to "school me" on the care of animals. (She didn't realize that morning had been particularly difficult for me as I was earlier informed of a death of a young lady who used to live with us).

So I drove up to the barn to get a trailer and then headed to the field to see what was going on. As I drove up to the animal, I noticed that it wasn't a horse; it was one of the llamas, Tony. He was thrashing in a puddle of water, banging his head against the ground, crying a wretched scream, having seizures, and struggling to breathe. Not a good sight, and hardly a situation with a good prognosis. I thought the best thing to do was to get him to the barn, where I could put him under a heat lamp. I tried to load him but couldn't lift him into the trailer by myself, so I called for help and continued my mud-wrestling to help get Tony into the trailer. I was frustrated and tearful as I knew this scenario wasn't going to have a good ending. As I was waiting for help to arrive and struggling to get this dearly loved animal into the trailer, I looked up and saw a car on the highway—it was Cindy in her white SUV, on the phone probably reporting me to the "llama police."

Covered in llama dung, urine, mud, and blood, and sitting on the trailer straining to get this animal drug up into the trailer, a thought came to me: *I don't need criticism and ridicule right now . . . what I need is help.* I didn't need judgment; I needed assistance. I didn't need a lesson; I needed an extra pair of hands. So as I tugged, pulled, and comforted this dying animal, I wished Cindy had gotten out of her comfortable, heated car and helped me.

The emotions of the day were overwhelming. Feelings of loss were already heavy on my heart that morning with the news of the young lady's death and continued throughout the afternoon with the death of Tony. Between those losses were feelings of helplessness, frustration, and anger—all aimed at Cindy for her insensitivity and her arrogant and indignant approach to my day's pasture experience. Why, she couldn't even tell the difference between a llama and a horse, and she felt like it was her role to chastise me. That sting of criticism infuriated me, and for months, I prayed for the opportunity to confront Cindy.

Now, before you get as frustrated at Cindy as I was, let me use this story to emphasize some points as it's a perfect example of parents today who strive to hold their kids to a higher standard and help them develop character and integrity in their life.

First, Cindy's *intentions* were good. She saw a need and took time out of her schedule to pull over and give me a call. Even though I only got her call that day, I have to admit that there were a few hundred other cars that passed that morning and didn't stop, because they didn't even notice the hurt animal. In retrospect, Cindy and I would probably connect in our love for animals. I think the core of her phone call was good. I believe she meant well.

Second, I think her *timing* was off. Had she called any other day, I might have taken her correction a little differently. She had no idea the grief I had already experienced that morning.

And third, she had no *understanding* of what was really going on. She had no idea that we allow our animals to finish their life on our property, and I had stayed up all night with a horse that died a month earlier and was with him when he died. She had no idea of how devoutly we had taken care of our llamas and how we had taken costly steps to protect them from the meningeal worm that eventually killed Tony. She didn't understand that I would never neglect, hurt, or treat our animals badly. That morning, she saw an animal in the field; I saw a dying pet I had cared for the past ten years.

I think we wanted the same thing, but our perspectives that day were light-years apart.

She thought she was helping me by calling and informing me of our struggling animal. She intended something good and did it in a way that got an animal some help. But she ruined the potential of a relationship without even knowing it. For her messages that were intended to help me were only heard as judgment pushing me to not wanting anything to do with her.

Good Intentions, Bad Timing

Many times, the good message that parents express to their kids is interpreted as judgment. Their *intentions* are good, but their *timing*

84

is off because their *understanding* of what their child is living through is limited. Well-intended parents sometimes create dividing walls between their family relationships rather than bridges that connect them with their children.

Unfortunately, the good message of parenting often gets lost in translation of intent. The friction in relationships caused by what is said versus what is actually heard many times ignites a war of words and lights a fuse to an explosive attitude that detonates and destroys the delivery of much-needed messages of wisdom, scriptural insight, and ethical discussion.

An example of this is when a well-intended parent takes the opportunity to share some wisdom and encouragement with a child only to have the child respond in such a way that the parent leaves thinking, *What did I say wrong? Did I miss something? What just happened here?* This parent is not wrong in having a desire to offer advice, give correction, and point his or her child in a better direction. That's not the real problem. The real problem lies in the way the child is interpreting the parent's intention. And that interpretation is happening because of the impending storm rolling into the child's life.

Parents must understand that the movement from elementary school to middle school marks a transition from a world of positive existence into an atmosphere of toxic remarks, negative influences, contaminated information, and venomous intentions that collectively take a toll on a child's emotion and perceptions. Your kids are not listening only to you anymore. They're now hearing a negative noise against a backdrop of the not-so-distant roar of a looming storm and know that the end of innocence is approaching.

Teen lightning is striking closer and claps of thunder draw your child's attention to the changing wind, reminding your teen of this impending change of season. They don't quite know how to push away the dark clouds entering their sunny tween life, so in an effort to protect themselves, they begin to close off entry points into their heart. The welcome mat to the door of your child's heart has now been removed and replaced with a hanging sign that shouts "Leave me alone!" It's a difficult change for kids, and it's an even tougher change for parents, because their once effective means of communicating is now backfiring on them.

For parents, understanding your child's changing world becomes crucial, and timing your message of help is critical. Without these two components, chances are your child might just interpret your message as one of judgment, moving her away from you, rather than understanding your intent to offer her help at a time she needs you the most. If you don't change your parenting style to accommodate the changing atmosphere of your child's life, your teen might begin to hear your message of encouragement and hope as a negative judgment and reminder of her inadequacies, inabilities, failures, and incompetence. Your attempts to help might position you as one who causes more pressure than one capable of relieving the weight and stress faced by the challenges of growing up.

And just like my response to Cindy and the judgment I felt in her attempt to help me, your child may want nothing to do with you when in actuality she needs you the most.

A Parenting Style That Fails

I see this parenting style backfire in two specific areas of a child's life. The first area is one where parents hold their kids to standards, principles, values, and certain morals that were taught during pre-adolescence in a relational setting where parents were the primary source of influence. In this setting, parents constantly remind their child to act, talk, and think in a certain way. These reminders come in the form of repetition, constancy, and taking advantage of every moment to teach kids the lessons of life.

Enter the adolescent years. As we've already discussed, your child is exposed to more. Parents are no longer the primary source of influence. The pressures mount. Many feel like they don't belong; many find they don't have the skills to tackle the world before them. Some get lost in their search for who they are, too many are confused as to how to put it all together. They don't need criticism, judgment, and ridicule; they need help. They don't need judgment; they need assistance. They don't need a lesson; they need help in taking what they've been taught and learning how to apply it to the new world they now live in. Here's the kicker. It doesn't happen with repetition, constancy, and finding every moment to teach.

Teens who are wrestling with new issues in life seldom need to hear what they need to do—they already know that. They also don't need to hear how they can do better. Many times *repetition* at this stage of development only reminds them of how they have failed or missed an opportunity to shine. And constant nagging, correction, and badgering often just pushes them away. Most of the time kids just need someone to listen to them; they don't need to hear another lesson, another teaching, or another class on how to do it better.

When parents fail in their attempt to understand what is really happening in their child's life, the timing of their well-intended comments leaves a child feeling judged.

The second area where many parents miss the opportunity for greatness in the life of their child is when they fail to understand the diversity of the peer relationships their child is developing. Chances are most kids have a racially diverse group of friends and a variety of relationships with acquaintances who will cause them to question what they've been taught in the process of developing their own belief system. Kids are exposed to other religions and may even develop friendships with those of different faiths, causing them to question who's right and who's wrong. Many will get to know kids who are homosexual or have a wide range of acceptable behaviors, and they'll wonder where these friends fit into the lessons they've been taught. Others will wander through issues of alcohol, tobacco, definition of marriage, sanctity of life, divorce, sexual boundaries, and politically dividing promotions that call into question many of the life truths they have been raised to believe.

Here's an example of this. Most teens understand their parents' view of homosexuality. This has been a debated topic for many years and appears to be an issue that is not going away for a long time. It's inevitable that your child will eventually know teens who say they are homosexual or bisexual. At that point, what your child believes might collide with what they feel in their relationship with this person. It's easy to be judgmental about a person and a way of life in theory. It's harder when you know and care for someone who practices this lifestyle. When push comes to shove, the relationship usually wins out and the belief gets thrown out. It's easy for kids to dismiss previously held beliefs when the confusion surrounding the integration of their faith into a world desperate for relationships is challenged or conflicted.

Offer Love, Not Judgment

It's at this point of their two worlds clashing that parents want to be involved in the lives of teens as they wrestle through the development of their faith. What I have found is that it's easier to speak truth into the life of a teenager when that truth is spoken in love. Another phrase I would use for *love* is the simple concept of being nice, not judgmental.

The effectiveness of your approach to your kids during their time of wrestling through issues in life will be determined by the temperature of your comments and the nonjudgmental position you take when engaging with them. Judging builds walls that keep truth and the messenger of the truth from being involved in the life of a child when a connection with a source of wisdom is greatly needed.

A man recently told me that his older kids all wanted nothing to do with him. He said he couldn't understand why they felt that way, as he's been teaching them the same way he has all their life. Sadly, each of his kids I've talked to have complained that their father is the most judgmental person they know. This father has good intentions, but his lack of understanding gave way to poor timing in his parenting approach. How I wish he had known the following:

- Sometimes a child just needs to think out loud to process and have someone listen without giving an opinion.
- Not every teachable moment needs to become a time of teaching.
- Asking kids, "Are you asking me a question or wanting my opinion?" is a wonderful way to respect the kids and offer

help rather than shove your opinion down their throat through lecture.

- He's taught his kids well and doesn't have to keep reminding his kids where they've blown it; they already know.
- He doesn't have to point out every way his kids can do things better.
- Despite his good intentions he's missing the heart of his kids, who long to have a relationship with him.
- His judgmental comments about controversial issues have moved his kids to ignore all the wisdom he shares in other conversations.
- In his heart he feels like he's fulfilling his parenting role; but in his kids' hearts, he's an extremely judgmental man and one to be avoided.

Truth with judgment pushes kids away; truth with relationship draws them to you.

>>> **Part Three** <<<

Parenting
Practices That
Really Work

10

Relating Is More
Important than Winning

I'm convinced that parenting kids is more than just an exercise in entertainment, improvement, and survival. And it's more than just the fulfillment of the challenge to move them from dependence to independence. I know the purpose of parenting is more than a boot camp of preparation for the wars they'll face in life. And it's more than a workout that produces an ability in your child to work out so that their children can learn how to work out, so that their children can do the same.

Parenting kids is about a relationship.

After decades of application of this message to teens and their families, these are some of the lessons I have learned from its application:

- A discipline problem is usually a relationship problem.
- A communication problem is often rooted in relationship issues.
- The lack of understanding between a parent and child is usually the result of a few cracks in the relationship foundation.
- Kids change through relationship, not from the exercise of authority.

- Small issues become big issues where there is no relationship.
- Conflict becomes an enemy between two people when a relationship is no longer present; and conflict is quickly resolved where relationships flourish.
- Lessons to be learned from each other are better taught when a bridge of relationships is formed between two people.
- Rules in your home not connected in relationship usually cause rebellion.
- A person best recognizes wisdom when there is a relationship.

There's no question that a relationship with your child, whether a tween preparing to enter adolescence or a teen in the throes of the challenging teenage years, is not only important but essential to their survival and your sanity. Relationship isn't the only thing that is important, but it is the most important thing.

Your Unique Role as Parents

Out of all the billions of people on this planet, God chose you to parent your child. It's true whether it is your birth-child, your adopted child, a grandchild who has come into your life, or one of the kids in your neighborhood. God has crossed your life with theirs for reasons beyond what any parent will ever know. That means you have unique insights, wisdom, talents, skills, and values to give your child. In a culture that offers excitement, attraction, and promises of entertainment, it's easy for parents to feel that they can't compete. But kids really do want more than glitz and glamour. As human beings created in God's image, we are hardwired to want things with intrinsic value; your teens are no different.

Dads, chances are, you're going to be the man in your daughter's life until you give her away to the man with whom she'll spend the rest of her life. Your involvement with her will shape her ideals about relationships with men and more than likely determine the types of interactions she has with others. While moms usually instill a sense of value into the life of a child, dads validate their existence. Leave or ignore your daughter and when she is old, she will still remember the scars from your lack of participation in her life.

And I'll just bet, Mom, that your relationship with your son will determine the type of woman he marries one day. You'll have the opportunity to help him become the man someone wants to share her life with. Because of you, he'll know compassion and empathy and develop sensitivity beyond what his manliness allows. Have a good relationship with him, and he will bring you years of blessings—for you will always be on his mind and in his heart until his dying day. Spend time correcting or ridiculing him, or do everything for him, and you'll force him to express his manhood unhealthily and never be happy with who he is as a man.

Dads, your relationship with your son is essential and a key influence in his development into a man of character. Withhold your blessing or your expression of approval for who he is and is to become, and the damage will be evident throughout his life. The message that he is your son with whom you are well pleased can usher into his life a world of contentment, and its suppression can haunt a man all the days of his life. Take care to ensure that he knows of your love for him. Make sure that of all the losses your son will experience in his life, you are not one of them.

Moms, you will teach your daughters how to love a man, how to love children, how to balance many things in life. Your service is contagious, your diplomacy is elegant, and your hospitality shows grace in action beyond measure. Your daughter needs you, your thoughts, and your support. She does not need your nagging, shaming, or dominance. Your role is to help her become her own woman.

And grandparents, what's your role in the life of your grandkids? The fun one! You get to eliminate all the stuff that didn't work with your kids and spend your time giving wisdom, love, and acceptance in a way that can't be felt from parents. Your grandkids desperately need you in their life. You have the chance to take advantage of your wealth, knowledge, time, and position to add flavor to their life. Do so to acknowledge their worth and to affirm the role that your kids are having in their life.

Parents don't have to constantly entertain or pacify their kids. In a world where everything is never enough, trying to impress or give too much will do nothing more than wear parents out. Instead, parents can fulfill their kids' foundational desires by offering wisdom, creating relationship, giving their time, imparting value, and sharing experiences together, thus cementing their relationship. Kids will never get all of those things from anyone or anywhere else. And these gifts trump anything the world has to offer. And it can only be offered by you.

Teens, as others, were created as relational beings, not just herd animals. They long to connect, to engage with one another, and to have meaningful relationships. When personal connections don't happen, social molding, the impartation of wisdom, and the validation of value and self-esteem instilled by parents don't happen. But what does happen is this—new doors of opportunity open for parents to walk into the life of their child. That "Leave me alone!" sign hanging on their door transforms into a welcome mat for those parents who have spent time developing a relationship with their child.

Unfortunately, many parents spend their time making sure their child is completing homework, achieving good grades, keeping his or her room clean, attending school activities, not having conflict, staying away from porn, not drinking alcohol, not becoming too independent, abstaining from sex, making curfew, not driving too fast, doing chores, getting to all the activities, becoming successful and career minded, staying out of trouble, getting along with siblings . . . whew! With all effort being channeled into these many areas, it's no wonder that parents often don't have time to develop a relationship with their kids.

And if parents are running on the hamster wheel of activity to attain the "parent of the year" award, focusing on doing all the right parental things while forgetting about what their child might need the most, that door of opportunity for a meaningful relationship might just remain closed for a long time.

I'm not saying all these things are unimportant. Nor do I believe that they should be eliminated from parents' efforts in raising their children. I'm just saying that there may be something more important that needs to be cultivated. Can I meddle just a little bit more? You might be *doing* all the right things as a parent and not *being* what your child needs you to be for them. And if that's the position you find yourself in, I encourage you to evaluate your relationship with your child, look at what message they have hanging on the door of their lives, and make some changes in your own life to accommodate your child's longing to have a relationship with you.

Countering the effects of this culture won't happen by making sure your child's room is clean or ensuring that she makes good grades. It will happen across a bridge of relationship in which you don't stop pursuing, even if your child doesn't respond. To put it another way, it means you keep knocking at the door of your child's heart even when it gets shut in your face.

Commit to Spending Time with Your Kids

So here's what I suggest to every family I come into contact with. Find a place in your schedule that you can get with your child once a week, one-on-one. Make it over a breakfast, an afternoon meeting over coffee, or a special designated dinner that you can have consistently and systematically. Begin doing this when your child turns thirteen and let him or her know of your commitment to get together every seven days just to spend time with your child. It's better to start early with this tradition. Waiting to meet with your kids when there's conflict is like trying to string communication lines in the middle of a hurricane. Build those avenues now, when the "weather" is quiet, and build them in a way that they'll survive any storm that comes into your family.

When you get together, commit to not sharing your opinion unless asked, pledge (to yourself) not to correct language, thoughts, comments, or opinions, and be determined to get to know your child, their thinking, and their personality over the next few years. Parents ask me continually what I think would help get their child, soon-to-be teen, and hopefully soon-to-be adult through the adolescent years. This is it.

They should spend time developing a relationship with their

child and create a safe place at that weekly table that affords the opportunity to speak into their life.

While it can be too early to begin if your child is younger than ten, it's never too late, and eventually, always welcomed. Meet with your teen or preteen when things are going well, and make sure you counter your feelings and continue to meet when things aren't going so well, even if the time is spent in silence. Your presence sends the message, *I want to hang out with you in the good times, and I'm there for you in the bad times.* And your presence in and attentiveness to their life keeps you from being blindsided by the effects of the turbulent years of adolescence.

Your Weekly Time with Your Child

Just as you would set up a time to get with your clients, coworkers, or employees, do the same for your child. And granted, you might spend the first six months hearing about the TV shows they're watching, what other kids are doing, how they're frustrated with siblings, and what they want for Christmas. But one day, you will be sitting across the table with your child, and they'll begin the conversation and ask, in so many words, how to manage their life through this culture of confusion and have conversation that will one day address those difficulties that they encounter in life. You have to set the schedule. You have to create that atmosphere that is safe for your child to talk and comfortable for your child to share their heart.

If you're starting this late in their teen years, then give some encouragement for them to participate. If they don't want to, make it have a consequence that makes it worthwhile to get with you.

And meet regardless of the struggles going on at home. Maybe they were grounded the night before. Or maybe you guys argued over something. Still go and get together. They'll eventually see the benefit of spending this time together and will one day speak about it in their adult years.

These are the rules of engagement I have in place when I meet with kids:

- Let this be a time that you focus on them. It's not a time for you to bring a whiteboard, a Bible, or a self-help book. It's simply a time to connect.
- Share something about yourself that's not about how great you are or what lessons you learned (unless they ask), but more just about you. Show your child that you are human, you made mistakes, and you didn't have it all together when you were younger.
- It's okay to share your heart in short bits of conversation, not long lectures or diatribes that could be interpreted as judging them or their friends.
- You don't always have to be right. And you don't always have to know the answer.
- A discussion doesn't always have to have a period at the end of it. Remember, you and your child are getting together again the next week, and seven days of thinking and praying might just give you some insightful wisdom that would be more welcomed.
- It's okay to let your child "win" in a discussion once in a while. If not, he'll quit discussing.
- Don't ever use this opportunity to criticize or "dress down" (yelling and berating until one is reduced to tears and

acknowledge their failings) your child. That will only keep interaction from happening in the future.

- Your acknowledgment of your shortcomings creates an environment in which they can share theirs. You're looking for opportunities to speak truth into their life, not to judge everything they say or to point out inconsistencies in their character.
- Likewise, don't judge their comments. This is a hard one, as it's hard to listen to foolishness when you have so much wisdom. Patience is the key here. Your time will come once you have created an atmosphere of openness.

At first, your conversations will likely be chitchat about what they watched that day on television, who said what on Facebook, what they want for their birthday, what you can get for them that day, or how much their brothers and sisters are bugging them. But in time, your conversations will progress into opportunities for them to begin sharing their heart. Give it time. The constancy of times spent together ensures your presence in their life at the time that they need you the most.

Here are some objectives to focus on during your weekly meeting.

The Sharing of Wisdom

Sharing wisdom is the communication of the right principles of living based upon experience, knowledge, and sound judgment. I know for me that the sharing part doesn't always come so easy. It's something that I have to pray about, think about, and spend some time doing some homework about before I can weave wisdom into the stories of my life.

Don't let this opportunity you have with your child turn into a setting where you tell them what *not* to do in life; they'll eventually want to quit meeting. Let it be a time that you are focused on sharing personal experiences that would convey wisdom. Share your failures, your mistakes, and problems you've encountered. From that platform, then share what you learned and what the application was that got you to a better place. Don't lecture your child. Have a conversation.

Your child needs wisdom that is shared in a way that gives him hope and a future; and you are the one to share that with him.

If they don't get wisdom from you, they'll search for it somewhere else.

The Opportunity for Relationship

Whenever I engage with parents or teens, I look for a commonality that allows conversation that allows a relationship to form. In your first meeting with your child, ask what you have in common and then follow up with a question about how you are different. Remember, don't share your opinion unless asked, and don't criticize in the way your child responds. Don't tell her that her opinion is wrong. Look for points of interests, common likes and dislikes, shared feelings, and genuine interests—all in the form of a question. Kids are smart enough to know when you are asking questions to gather information so that you can "nail" them for doing something wrong.

Before you spend time meeting, make a list of stories in your life where you learned something. And keep a running log of thoughts, lessons, and mistakes that you've made in your life. Those always come in handy at the right time to accentuate a point that you want to get across should the question ever get asked.

Tell a story. Everyone loves stories. But tell it in a way that's entertaining and keeps their interest. Don't be judgmental. The older your kids get, spend time talking and discussing current events, political views, social concerns, and spiritual debates. Learn to say, "I don't know," "I've never thought about that," and "You'll have to ask someone else about that one." Make learning fun. And make sure they know that by the end of the time that they've had with you that day that you are someone that they'd like to spend more time with.

It's all about relationship.

If they don't have a relationship with you, they'll have one with someone else.

The Giving of Time

Time is funny. It's gone before you know it. And you'll be sending that little kid off to college or helping her move into an apartment. It passes quickly so take advantage of the time you have.

Your child's teenage years may not be the time to be involved in so many other things. Perhaps the position of being an elder at the church can wait. Maybe the neighborhood association can find someone else to lead this go-around. Maybe that golf game every Saturday can be given up to pour time into the life of your child. Maybe the time you pour into others can be put on the back burner as you pour your life into your child. There will always be time in the future to serve the church, play golf, and be involved with others. But there won't be that many years before your child leaves home.

Time is a funny thing, isn't it?

If they don't spend time with you, they'll spend it with someone else.

A Concept of Value

Set aside a time that you dedicate not to criticize or correct your teen, but instead to provide a safe atmosphere in which your child knows, no matter what's going on at the moment, that you love them dearly. In school, they're being told how they can always do better. In activities, there's always competition. At home, are they always being corrected or told how to do things better?

I suggest that there be a place in the life of your child that he knows he will not be judged, competing, corrected, or criticized. The fact that you are spending time out of your schedule lets your child know that you value him. So don't blow it as an opportunity to just give them more of what they get everywhere else. Value is determined by the importance you place on this time together. That value should be reflected by the number of times you get together, the time that you show up (physically and mentally), the atmosphere you create, how you let them get what they want, and the way you engage with them.

End each weekly meeting with your child with this phrase: "There's nothing you can do to make me love you more, and there's nothing you can do to make me love you less." You'll know this truth is being seared on their heart when your child says, "I know Dad (or Mom), I know."

If you don't give them value, they'll get value from someone else.

A Chance for Experience

When you spend time together, look for opportunities to experience more together. If your daughter mentions that she's always wanted to jump out of a plane, then make plans to do it together.

It will be a memory she will never forget. If your son says he's always wanted to attend a sporting event, then make plans to do that with him. Experience the moment where your child not only gets to hear you; she gets to see you in action. Think out of the box. Go to New York City, buy a dog, jump out of a plane, go on a hunting trip, go to Disney World, experience the Smithsonian, go on a fishing trip, attend a concert, or stay up late to watch a meteor shower with a campfire and hot chocolate. Go fishing, build something together, and take a vacation of a lifetime while you still have life and they still have time.

The moods of a lifetime are often found in the never-to-be-forgotten experiences of the teen years. Make sure that you're a part of those experiences.

If they don't do things with you, they'll do things with someone else.

What is a once-a-week meeting with your child worth?

Everything.

It's a win-win deal for both of you.

11

Ask Questions to
Create Connections

o you ever wonder if your child will be one of the casualties of the current adolescent culture? Do you worry that while you have had the skills to get your child through their elementary school years that you might not have the parenting skills to help them during their middle school and high school years? Do you think that there might be things happening in the life of your child that you don't know about, just as your parents didn't know about everything that happened in your life?

Do you feel like you no longer truly know your child and what he or she is thinking about and dreaming of?

These questions have got you thinking a little bit, haven't they? Scared about the answers? Are you fearful about the possibilities? Concerned for your child? Are you frightened of that approaching storm as well?

Questions have a mighty way of getting you to think outside the box and consider something other than what you have been holding onto for comfort or out of habit. They arouse you to think. And in the process of that thinking, you either rely on the resources you have collected throughout your life to answer some of those questions or you search for answers from people around you who can give insight, wisdom, and some knowledge outside of your understanding. If you accept their counsel, chances are it helps you in your journey of answering the unanswered uncertainties you encounter. The gathered knowledge of the principles of right living (wisdom) gained in the past, coupled with the influence of knowledgeable relationships around you keeps you on the path you were intended to walk.

Your child is no different.

Every week I'm asked how I communicate with kids. I'll tell you how this white-mustached grandpa gets kids to talk to me and to come back for more. I ask questions, seldom give my opinion, and am careful with my answers. Let me break this down for you.

The Value of Questions

Asking questions does a couple of things that are crucial in developing a relationship of longevity with your child. First of all, it makes them feel valued. Do you think kids in their tween and teen years need to experience a sense of worth in a world of performance and appearance? The unadulterated inquiry into their life from you conveys a sense of interest that is seldom displayed and rarely seen by others. I think it impresses a teen to think that someone from a different world would want to come into theirs and show an interest about their life, no matter how put together or how messed up it is.

For your teen to feel this value, you must position and communicate questions in a way that does not make your teen interpret your question as

- another form of interrogation where you're digging up dirt or trying to find evidence of wrongdoing;

- a courtesy question just to give you a platform to share another one of your opinions;
- an inquiry to gather information to be used at a later date to prove a point;
- an attempt to jump into their life to add another improvement to their "makeover list";
- a sarcastic remark parked in a question that passes judgment;
- an accusatory investigation into the habits, choices, and actions of friends.

While there may be an occasion in which you have to ask questions to accomplish the things I've listed above, there must be a time and place or opportunity where your teen feels safe and your questions are focused to gain insight into your child's heart. Teens will sense the genuineness and authenticity of your concern; they know if it's real or not.

Second, asking questions gives teens the opportunity to share answers that show you where their interests are, where their confusion is seated, what conflict of values they might be struggling with, and why they're behaving the way they are. Questions are the keys that unlock the door of opportunity to engage deeply with your teen and allow motives, hurts, and hidden feelings to rise to the surface. This is what you want, isn't it?

Your questions should then be derived from the answers your teen gives and the follow-up questions he asks of you. If you spend your time asking questions, you may hear more than you want, and you'll likely hear some things that you'd rather not know. But I can guarantee this: you'll never have a shortage of topics to discuss.

I don't share my opinion with teens I'm counseling unless I am asked for it—and then only rarely. Remember the point of asking questions isn't so that *we* can find the answer; it is so *they* can find the answer. And I'm not so sure that my opinion about a particular topic sticks to the ceiling when tossed to and fro in a teenager's life as much as an opinion that is self-formulated through their search for the truth. I don't want a child to mimic or duplicate my opinions. I want them to go further and deeper in developing their own opinions. This style makes for some interesting discussions and varied opinions that in the long run will indeed reflect my influence, but not necessarily my exact feelings about a particular issue or topic. How boring would it be to sit around and talk with people who all feel exactly the same way that you do about everything? I might as well be talking to a mirror.

So when the look in a kid's eye says, *Hey, I need some help here,* and I can tell that his wheels are turning, I usually ask, "Do you want an answer or are you asking my opinion?" There are times he just says, "Neither." And I respond, "Okay." Then there are times that a teenager says, "Give me your opinion." More times than not, I respond by saying, "I'm not sure what I think about that"—not because I really don't know, but because I don't want to stop the teen from formulating his own opinion. On rare occasions, I let him know what I think.

Why? It is because I want teens to continue to question and search with their whole heart. I want them to keep thinking. I want them to take those bits of truth they've already been taught and figure out how to place them in their faith and value development. I want them to do it, instead of me acting like I have to do everything for them. I want them to come up with the answer rather than take the lazy way out and have something given to them. I want them to feel proud for what they've done, not for what they've been told. I want them to develop their own thoughts and beliefs, not just plagiarize mine. I want to be the one who directs them to truth, not the one who gives them all the truth.

Do you see the necessity of changing your parenting style of teaching from lecture to discussion and filling that discussion with questions?

Answers

I am amazed at the stars. I love meteor showers. I get up early or stay up late just to see a passing comet, or something funky happening with the moon. I look for shooting stars, have seen the moons around Jupiter, get intrigued about the pulsating expansion of the universe, and read any article about astrophysics I can. I am filled with wonder about the universe because I can't understand it all. It's that wonderment that keeps me looking. The beauty and intrigue beyond this earth for me happens because I don't know the answers to most of the questions I have about the solar system. Until I get to heaven, I'll keep enjoying what I see and live with a great sense of contentment that I don't have to know everything.

The questions you ask your teens should pique their interest, not satisfy their curiosity. The amazing expedition of understanding and realization is a lifelong road trip where the joy is in the journey, not in its completion.

I believe that teens often don't search for many answers because they feel like they have them all. They don't marvel at much because everything has been explained away. And most like fish, but many don't know how to catch them.

Questions have an amazing way of getting us to think, don't

they? They set the wheels of intrigue and interest in a motion that immediately stops when the answer is found. Kids don't need more answers; we live in a world of information that can explain away many things. And parents feel that if they just give the right answers and keep filling their kids with more facts, solutions, appropriate responses, remedies, and repair techniques, then all would be perfect. Right? How boring!

A Groundwork of Questions

I encourage you to quit trying to figure out how to give all the answers to your tweens and teens and start engaging and responding to them in ways that help them find solutions. My communication with kids is not built on a foundation of answers but on the groundwork of questions. Here are some of my responses to questions and comments kids ask that I utilize to keep the conversation going and create a world of thinking, wonderment, and searching:

- "Wow, that must have been tough . . . was it?"
- "You think so?"
- "Is that working for you?"
- "Did you come up with that yourself, or did someone tell you that?"
- "Is that a good thing?"
- "I can't see that working in my world . . . how does it work in yours?"
- "Is that going to get you where you want to be?"
- "Man, where did that thought come from?"

Here's a key to my communication. My hope is to build a relationship with teens that promotes interaction and communication that will last for years. As a result, I know that I'll have plenty of times to revisit comments, ask more questions, dig a little deeper, and be part of their development. In other words, I don't have to fix everything in that one setting, and it is not essential to give the right answer each time.

Want to know how you can usher in an era of asking questions in your family? The first step is to learn not to be afraid of silence. Even a fool appears wise when he keeps his mouth shut (Proverbs 17:28). Another proverb warns, "Seldom set foot in your neighbor's house, lest he become weary of you and hate you" (Proverbs 25:17). Put these two proverbs together and apply them to communicating with your soon-to-be or current teen, and the lesson would be this: talk less so your teens will come to you, and don't talk too much or they'll cut you off quickly.

I've found that many parents consistently feel the need to remind a teen what to do, how to do it, and whether she did it right. It's almost as if they don't trust what they've taught their child so they have to keep teaching, reminding, and repeating lessons to such a point that a child eventually shuts down, hoping the parent will shut up. The bad part about this is that the child then misses out on the golden nuggets of wisdom that parents share because there is so much "noise" coming her way.

Moms and dads . . . stop! If you want your tweens and teens to start moving toward you, then stop pushing yourself on them, especially in communication. If you want to know the intensity of your approach, stop talking for a day and see the reaction you get from your kids. I think you'll find that they'll start moving toward you, asking questions all along the way. The first question will be, "Dad, what's wrong with Mom? She's not talking." And your answer should be, "I don't know. Why don't you ask her?" (not sarcastically). Just ask questions—don't give an answer. I think you'll be amazed at their response.

A Simple Exercise in Listening

Once you spent a few days backing down on the number of words that are spoken by you or your spouse, try this little exercise at the dinner table. Just ask a simple question: "What is most important to you?" The ground rules are simple. Everyone must answer, and dessert isn't served until everyone gives at least five things that are important to him or her. And if you need to, encourage them. Tell them that you'll give them something if they answer with something more than a shrug of the shoulders, a one-word answer, or can dig deep and come up with something special to them. I'd give them each some cash. Hey, you're going to give all your money to them one day anyway, so you might as well give it now so you can get something out of it! Encouragement through reward is a good way to get them to interact. Eventually, they'll understand your questions and might enjoy being heard when they share their opinions. (For conversation starters, see appendix A.)

And when they answer, listen. Don't share your opinion until asked. And even if asked, you don't always have to answer. Don't judge their comments, and don't try to tell them how to say something better or how to communicate better. Just listen. You might find out something about your child you never knew. And you'll have plenty of time to communicate in the future if they know the dinner table is a safe place to connect with you.

Can you see how conversations full of questions have a more powerful influence on a young teen than those filled with lecture and directives? Fill your discussions with your kids with questions. It creates an internal world of wonderment and journeying that is self-motivated (by them) rather than outwardly stimulated (by you). Teens need to learn to ask questions, and that will only happen as they observe your wise example.

>>> 12 <<<

Stop Controlling and Start Trusting

A parent recently called and asked if I would meet with her concerning her seventeen-year-old son. He was being antagonistic at home, engaging in some inappropriate behavior, copping an attitude with everyone in the family, and had become disobedient, dishonest, and disrespectful. The mother stated she didn't know why their son was acting up as she and her husband were loving parents, had been diligent in lining out all the expectations for the family, and had raised their kid "right."

When both parents came into my office, the mother proudly showed me a four-page list of requirements for their family. She said it was each person's choice to live by this list, but if they didn't choose it, they couldn't live at home. I looked over the list and was surprised at the length of the compilation and the detail of each entry. Here is a portion (30 out of the 120 listed items) of directives given to her son:

- Date Christians only, and only hang out with Christian kids.
- Pray daily and go to church—this is an integral part of your life.
- Do chores promptly with cheerful, positive attitude.
- Have at least one hobby you are always doing.

- Read a minimum of two books a month.
- Sundays are for family time—rest and visit.
- Don't get in a rut.
- Strive to be in a leadership position.
- Learn to have healthy relationships.
- Plan tomorrow the night before—it helps you be productive.
- Eat four fruits and five vegetables a day.
- Eat no more than one dessert a week.
- Maximum intake of red meat two times a week.
- Exercise three times a week for forty-five minutes.
- Drink eight glasses of water (8 oz.) each day.
- Keep yourself physically, mentally, and spiritually in shape.
- No sex before marriage and no fast women.
- No tobacco or alcohol ever.
- No reckless driving.
- Don't whine or play a victim.
- Pick your friends with caution.
- Be grateful—write thank-you notes to anyone who gives you something.
- Shower daily—nobody likes a stinky person.
- Brush and floss your teeth two times a day.
- Smile—it makes everyone feel better.
- Happiness is a choice, so choose to be happy.
- Tell parents "good morning" and "good night" with a hug and a kiss.
- Dream big, sacrifice, work hard, and don't quit.
- Dedicate yourself to schoolwork, projects, and work, and the Lord.
- No porn, no horror movies, and limit TV to five hours per week.

As I read the list, one word kept coming to my mind: *Wow!* Dad sat there with arms crossed with a look of disappointment in his son that could be seen the minute he walked in the building, and Mom sat waiting to hear what their son's problem was so I could give them the solution to correct it.

After talking with the parents a few more minutes, I said that I would like to meet with their son. As he came in the door, he was polite, cordial, and extremely engaging. When I asked him what had been going on, he pulled the four-page document out of his back pocket, tossed it on the table, and said, "This!" I felt a hint of humor while thinking that this document meant one thing to one person—and something entirely different to another.

When I asked the son what he thought about this 120-point collection of expectations, he emphatically but calmly stated, "My parents try to control everything in my life. Everything I do right is under their control so the only way that I can show any sort of control in my life, is to do some not-so-good things that are beyond their control. I'd rather do wrong and be in control than do right and not be in control."

That word came back to my mind: *Wow!* Out of the mouth of this young man came words that every parent could learn from.

In all fairness to the parents in this situation, I have to say that all the points these parents listed in their family belief system are good things and were well intended. There wasn't anything on the list that any parent wouldn't want for their kids. These parents put quite a bit of thought into determining what they wanted for their kids and putting it on paper so that all would understand. I applaud them for that. But somewhere in the presentation, something so well intended went terribly wrong because the interpretation was not what Mom and Dad hoped it would be. This young man heard the word *control* and wasn't about to let anyone derail his pursuit of gaining control of his life. This document was presented one way but interpreted an entirely different way.

A Longing for Control

This young man is no different than any other kid I've known my whole life. And whether teens are more immature now than in years past, it doesn't matter. The longing for teens to be in control of their life is as old as dirt.

I met with a group of kids a few weeks ago and asked them, "What do you think about your parents controlling you?" Here are some of their responses:

- "My parents and I were fighting, but for two different things. They were fighting for protection; I was fighting for control."
- "They wouldn't let me do anything and they would never give me a reason why . . . I kept thinking, 'I'm eighteen and they treat me like I'm twelve.'"
- "They never trust me to do anything, so I started to take control of my life behind their back."
- "I started smoking just to prove to my parents that it was one area of my life they didn't control. And when they grounded me for smoking, I felt good because I knew I was in control of my life."
- "I wanted to prove to my parents that they couldn't control me . . . I think that's why I tried to kill myself."
- "I felt alive when I was in control and everyone except my parents knew me as one who could be in control."

- "My parents are control freaks. They trust no one . . . They'll never trust me, so I quit listening to them long ago."
- "The tighter they clamped down, the more I wanted to fight back. Most of the problems I have in life are because of my parents. They didn't train me; they ruined me. All because they wanted to be in control."

Do you think kids want to be in control of their life? Of course they do. And deep down, I think we as parents would all say that we want them to be. Yet somewhere there is a breakdown between thought and action. I think this is why.

Adolescents tend to be focused on themselves. Many wake up every morning with an attitude that says, *What's in it for me?* In an effort to combat their teens' self-focus, parents take control and try to prove to their teenagers that the world does not revolve around them. They teach their teens that they need to think of others, they are not in control, they will submit to authority, and they are going to learn to respect being told what to do.

So in an attempt to help their teens become more considerate of others and rid them of their self-centered mentality, parents take control. And they take control in more ways than just limiting privileges or taking away objects of desire to show consequences for inappropriate behavior. Control of your child can be shown through threats, name-calling, blaming, ridicule, mind games, jealousy, sarcasm, manipulation, isolation, economics, domination, intimidation, and verbal and physical assaults. When parents exert control through these means, it's not hard to predict the outcome.

Parents then battle against this self-centered mentality, and their kids interpret it as an assault on their control. So the battle begins, and usually it's the parents who lose. I've said for years that I've only met about five or six kids in the thousands I have dealt with whom I would say are truly rebellious. All the others have been responding to difficult situations in their life, such as fighting for control.

Parents, your child's "It's all about me" attitude will take care of itself one day through social interaction, teachers' directives, a boss's comment, or just natural consequences. The battle of helping a child realize his or her self-focus is just a small skirmish compared to the war that could develop from not giving territorial control.

Who Makes the Choices?

When it comes to making choices in their lives, teens want three things. They want to make decisions about themselves. They want to feel like they're in control. And they want opportunities to prove their maturity and show parents that they can do it.

Don't you want the same? You do because you want your child to make a good choice about a spouse. You want them to be able to choose which direction to take when confronted with alternatives. You want them to say no because it's a good decision, and not to say yes just to prove to you that they can make decisions for themselves. You want them to be in control enough to choose the right path when some young man wants to sleep with your daughter or when your son is offered the opportunity to smoke pot. You want your teens to take control of their own choices, because you don't want to control them when they leave home.

They'll learn to make decisions when you give them the

opportunity to make their own choices at a young age. Begin at twelve, and increasingly give them more decisions each year. Then, when they reach eighteen, they'll be making decisions on their own. They may come to you to seek wisdom on what decision to make, but the plan must be to have them making all their decisions so they're ready to take that next step of life. Start early transferring control so your children get to practice making decisions. The more practice they get, the better they'll be at making decisions later when the repercussions of those decisions are greater and potentially more damaging.

So quit controlling, and start trusting.

Concerns about Giving Teens Choices

When it comes to giving kids the freedom to make their own choices, are you afraid your children will make mistakes? Sure they will. It will give you plenty to talk about, but don't shame them. Use their mistakes as an opportunity to help them make better decisions in the future. Allow the results of a foolish decision to be their teacher. Don't rescue them from the consequences of poor judgment. Too often, parents are so afraid their child might make a life-damaging mistake that they don't let their kids do the hard work of growing up. To maintain order and pursue a steady course, parents often try to control their children's lives. Then they complain that their teens are lazy, irresponsible, and unmotivated.

Do you think your kids aren't ready to make their own choices? Of course they're not. The only way they will be ready is for you to give up control a little bit at a time, thus giving them control at the same pace so they can become ready. Don't force them to have to rebel to gain control of new territory that will eventually be theirs.

Do you think your teen will get hurt if you give him control of his life? I've never met a teen who hasn't felt hurt from a decision that didn't turn out the way he or she thought. But I've seen too many kids-turned-adults who are spinning out of control because they've never had control. That's why it's important for kids to start learning to make decisions early. The longer you wait to give them the opportunity to take control of their life, the greater the pain will be when one of their decisions backfires.

This is where overprotection hurts your child. When parents feel the need to protect a child from making immature decisions that could cause pain in their life, they end up delaying that decision-making to a later time when the consequences for poor decisions could have catastrophic and lifelong effects. Overprotection really isn't protection at all. Many times, parents' desire to protect their child supersedes the greater need to prepare their child for the world in which they will live. And it centers on giving them control of their life.

Kids are resilient. They adapt. They learn quickly. They want to be in control of their life. They want to make decisions. They want to make you proud. They want to live up to your expectations. But they want to do it with them being in control, not you.

Three Areas of Trust

The greatest roadblock for parents in turning control over to your child is usually an issue of three areas of trust. First, trusting your kids is tough. Teens will make poor choices. They will wreck the car. They will lie when pushed into a corner. They will make mistakes. They will blow it many times. They will get angry. They will say things they wished they hadn't. And they won't always treat people the way they should. But just because they don't do everything perfectly doesn't mean that we shouldn't give them the opportunity to take control of their lives.

Here's something you *can* trust: teenagers will act like teenagers during their teenage years.

Second, trusting what you have taught your kids is paramount. The fact that you're reading this book speaks volumes to the probability that you've taught your kids well during their elementary school years. Now start trusting that all those seeds you have sown into the life of your child will come to fruition. Know that the truths your kids have learned will always eventually win out. Trust what you've done.

Third, trusting God's involvement in your kids' life is imperative. God wants good things for your child. And just as He will never leave us, He will never leave them (Hebrews 13:5). In your absence, God will be there for them, reminding them of all the lessons you have taught and encouraging them to choose wisely.

Make a plan today to entrust one decision every few months to your child and let your teenager make more and more decisions concerning her life and her future. Start with little things and progress to larger decisions. Sure, you have to set parameters and boundaries, but try to find a way to let your child know that your intent is to transfer control gradually from you to her. And present these boundaries to her in a way that she knows that your desire is for her to take control of her life, and not about you wanting to control her.

When your children, even at age twelve, begin to understand that you are *for them* making decisions, and *for them* taking control of their life, and *for them* developing their independence, and *for them* making good choices, and *for them* showing you how they can do it, you'll have kids who respond to your correction, input, wisdom, and relationship in a way that draws them to you.

13

Foster Independence

One day, your precious daughter will walk out your door and life will never be the same, as she is no longer under your rule. Or it may be a son who leaves home and heads to college, the military, or a new job, and you know his boyhood days are over. At that moment, it won't matter whether his room is clean, the condition of her bathroom, whether he came in by curfew, or what music she was listening to. It won't matter if he watched too much TV, played too many video games, made some mistakes along the way, or whether she didn't study as much as she should have. What will matter is whether your child is still dependent on you to make it in life or whether your relationship with her has helped her develop the skills she needs to stand firm against what she will encounter in the next chapter of her life.

Chances are you have longed for a better relationship with your child than you had with your parents. And greater chances are that you have given your child more than you were ever given. There is something about having a relationship with your child that makes every parent a little protective because they don't want to lose a child in the next chapter of life. I also believe that many parents lavish a great number of gifts and desired things upon their kids. When parents have a need for a relationship (not just a "want") that is coupled with a desire to give things to their child to affirm that relationship, the mixture of the two provides an unhealthy environment unless parents are very careful.

A Necessary Shift in Parenting Style

I, too, wanted a better relationship with my kids than I had with my parents. And I wanted to give them things, maybe because I wanted to outdo what my parents did for me in hopes of maybe trying to be a better parent. What I found was that so much of what I thought I was doing for my kids, I was really doing for myself. I was getting something from the relationship, and I was getting value from having them be dependent on me.

Somewhere along the line of raising kids, there must be a shift in a parenting style that quits providing everything for a child and helps them learn to provide for themselves.

I'm not saying that you should quit giving your twelve-year-old gifts and money and make them head out to get a job, but I am saying that the move from total dependence to total independence should be in the forefront of all your actions as your child heads into the adolescent years. What you do during this time to help them become independent will determine how successful they are in the next chapter of their life, including work, marriage, children (your future grandkids), and adulthood. This mind-set is having their interests as your focus.

I'm also not saying that you should cut off your children at age eighteen and make them fend for themselves. But I am saying that an eighteen-year-old would be better off having a concept that you are not obligated to provide for him and you owe him nothing . . . and want to give him everything. This mind-set forces a desire on his part to begin to develop skills that will allow him to make the transition into successful adulthood and puts you in a position of offering and helping, rather than giving them a sense of entitlement. The mind-set is far better adapted to a parenting style when a child is headed into junior high school than deciding to give your child a quick crash course on "How to be Independent in Six Months" right after they turn eighteen.

My hope is that parents will move a preteen toward independence in a way that moves her to developing responsibility for her life and move away from depending on you for their existence—and to have this process begin at age twelve.

Why? Because your child at age twelve has six more years of living with you and has ten times that number of years ahead to live apart from you. So quit focusing on pleasing, protecting, and providing for your child, and shift your focus to preparing your child to leave home and not be dependent on you! Kids have a natural desire to be dependent on their parents as long as the parents provide. Provision quickly moves to enabling if your actions don't wean them from their necessity for and dependence upon you as years pass.

Failure to Launch

If you have a twenty-one-year old living at home who isn't motivated to find a job, do something with his or her life, or get off the couch, sometimes outer motivation is required where an inner drive lacks. Even if you didn't foster independence in your child as he grew through his teen years, your mistake (or in fact, any blunder) should not give your child license to continue a sense of entitlement and not develop independence. You're not helping your child by allowing him to do nothing. That's where the terms for these kids have become common.

- A *boomerang kid* comes back home because he can't function in the world he is to live in.
- A twenty-something is caught in *waithood*, waiting for adulthood to happen.
- A *parasite single* sucks the life from Mom and Dad because she just doesn't want to be independent.
- A *twixter* (one caught betwixt adolescence and adulthood) justifies his existence by blaming it on the economy, on politics, or social influences.
- Young men and women caught in *emerging adulthood* complain of having a *quarter-life crisis*, so they become *NEETs*—Not in Education, Employment, or Training.
- In Japan, these kids are called *freeters*, and in Mexico and Spain they're called *ni-ni*—"neither study, nor work" *(ni estudia, ni trabaja)*.

I understand kids living at home for economic reasons, medical issues, or being in transition, but I don't agree with the concept of having a child live at home because he couldn't launch. If a child can't launch, nine times out of ten, a parent hasn't done a good job in helping that child become and maintain her independence. Immaturity, coupled with a sense of entitlement, saturated with irresponsibility and the inability to make decisions, point more toward a parent's lack of training than a child's fault. To expand on an earlier statement, a child's ability to make decisions, whether good ones or bad ones, is usually determined by a parent's willingness to let that child make decisions and embrace the need for making good decisions when consequences for bad choices are allowed to have their full effect.

Here's an easy directive that is hard to implement but is necessary to fostering independence in your children as they learn to take control of their life: let them make decisions and be there to guide and direct the decision-making process.

Years ago, I met with a nineteen-year-old young man at the request of concerned parents who weren't happy with his lack of motivation and seeming lack of desire to get a job, go to school, make money, and live on his own. Within five minutes of us sitting down, I asked him why he thought his parents wanted me to meet with him. In an arrogant tone he told me that he didn't see any reason to meet, because he was doing fine. His exact words were: "I get three meals a day, have shelter over my head, I'm comfortable, and my parents love me. What more could I want? They want me to go to college or get a job, but I don't need either." I knew immediately what the problem was and knew exactly how to fix it.

I later told the parents that their son would come to his senses when they quit giving him everything. Recently, this young man, who is now twenty-seven, got in touch with me on Facebook and asked if we could get together. The minute we sat down, he asked, "Remember the first time we got together?" We laughed out loud reminiscing about his cockiness. He said, "That was my wake-up call. If it wasn't for that call, I don't think I would be married or have the two beautiful kids that I do. And I think when we buried my mother last year, she would have gone to her grave being so disappointed in me. Thanks!"

How to Foster Independence in Your Child

Here's how you begin to foster independence as your child begins to enter the teen years. Tell your child that you're going to initiate a new plan on the following date:

- "On *New Year's Day*, we're going start something new in our family . . ."
- "On your *birthday* this year, it will be a new time of allowing you to make more decisions for your life."
- "On *Labor Day*, you're going to have to get a job."
- "On *Independence Day*, you're going to have to pick up what I will no longer be doing . . . and become more independent."
- "It's *Memorial Day*, and we're going to memorialize what we've been doing and start out on a new path."
- "This *Christmas*, I'm going to give you a gift that will allow you to become more independent."
- "This *Halloween*, we're going to do something that may sound scary, but I believe it will be helpful to you."
- "On *April Fool's Day*, I'm going to let you start taking more control of your life; no joke!"
- "This *Thanksgiving*, we're going to celebrate giving because I want to, not because I have to."

They'll begin to understand that some things are going to change. What needs to change? Let me ask you. What are you doing for your kids that they can pick up and start doing for themselves? Not because you don't want to continue to help your child do these things, but because you need to let them start doing some things to help usher in the new years of fostering independence. Here are some things you can require from your children when they turn thirteen:

- Getting themselves out of bed with an alarm clock
- Picking out their own clothes every morning
- Getting ready for school and eating breakfast
- Getting to school on time
- Doing their own laundry
- Cleaning their own rooms (even if you have a housekeeper)
- Doing their homework without you having to nag them to do it
- Making their own snacks after school.

The point of the exercise is not taking away from your parenting role but changing your child-rearing role to now encompass training to help them learn to begin to take care of themselves. It's not less parenting; it's a different type of parenting.

As children get older, I encourage you to give them more things to do, more decisions to make, more opportunities for them to have to figure out what to do, and more opportunity to assume responsibility for their life. Here are some other training focus points you might want to consider.

- Handling finances
- Making good decisions
- Breaking the mind-set of entitlement
- Keeping relationships when there's conflict
- Handling stress and resolving disagreements
- Not always having to be right

- What to do when you're wrong
- Treating a friend with kindness
- Finding the right spouse
- The value of a good day's work
- Setting objectives and working toward those goals
- Standing for what you believe
- Essentials of a disciplined life
- Integrity and keeping your word
- The need for community and the development of relationships
- Having fun and learning how to take care of yourself
- How to surround yourself with wise people
- Finding the job that fits your skill set
- Making money and living within your means
- Changing a tire on a car
- How to ask for help

You must break the entitlement mentality that has become a cultural influence. I would let teens know the following: "I owe you nothing, but I want to give you everything." When your children begin to see you as one who is giving because you want to, as one who will help them learn new ways of living with a goal of independence, and as one who is always thinking ahead, their response to you will be one of gratitude and respect.

Will your kids make mistakes? Sure they will. But they'll come to new conclusions about what to do when things don't turn out as planned. Know how I learned about rebuilding boats? I sunk one. Know how I learned about gas engines? I burnt one. Know how I learned about training horses? After getting bucked off too many. Know how I learned about relationships? By messing up a lot of them.

Know when I learned to make money? When I realized that I wasn't going to get it from anywhere else. Know when I trusted Christ? When I realized that I was in need. When children realize their need, they're resilient enough to come up with an answer. So don't bail them out; let them learn. It's a part of the training process.

You may hear some of the following comments from your kids along this path of independence:

- "I can do this on my own."
- "I don't need your help."
- "I can't wait to leave home."
- "I don't believe that way."
- "I don't agree with you."
- "I can make it on my own."
- "Thanks for the input, but I think I'll do it this way."
- "I blew it . . . Can you help me?"

Don't be so quick to interpret all these as rebellious comments. Most of the time, they're verbal affirmations that you're doing a good job in helping your child become independent. So don't ruin the opportunity to affirm their independence by saying things like, "I told you so," "That's a stupid thought," "That will never happen," or "I knew that would happen." Those kinds of statements don't foster independence but breed dislike and contempt.

Helping your child develop independence while still living at home fosters independence in your young adult's own thoughts, opinions, and actions. It will even benefit your grandchildren—who are more likely to have a mature parent, your son or daughter, caring for them.

14

Add Clear Boundaries
and Subtract Strictness

The mark of a good parent is not necessarily a well-behaved child. And a good kid isn't always one who never gets into trouble, makes a bad decision, or fails a class. I trust that a mark of good parenting is not only determined by the way a child acts at home during his or her teen years, but also how a child engages and lives during his or her later years. And sometimes the healthiest one in the whole family can be the rebellious child. I state this because of the experiences that I've had with kids who have lived in our residential counseling center.

I've watched kids who behave wonderfully at home but have shared with me how much they hate their parents, can't wait to get away from them, and never want to see them again when they eventually leave their house. I've seen kids so isolated from the real world and so controlled by parents that they behave well in their younger years but are complete messes once they are on their own. I've seen the fear in the eyes of well-behaved kids when their parents approach, and it doesn't take a rocket scientist to figure out what's really going on back at the ranch. On two occasions, I've heard news that a child committed suicide, and upon hearing the news I was saddened yet not surprised.

I've had parents tell me when placing their child with us in our residential counseling center that the problem that resulted in their kid living on our campus isn't really the kid's fault. One dad told me, "I've been too controlling, too strict, and too hard on my child . . . and I think I've ruined her."

The common denominator in all these situations? Parents who are much too strict.

The Danger of the Authoritarian Approach

When parents are strict and in control, many kids are well behaved yet feel a deep contempt for their parents. And if provoked enough through limitations, isolation, authoritarian discipline, and exasperating sternness, teenage angst can quickly turn to intentional disobedience and focused disrespect. Many kids will eventually express their anger of not getting what they want by violating everything a parent has taught or desires for a child, just to show Mom and Dad who is really in control.

As I mentioned in chapter 8, I don't have faith in the authoritarian approach to parenting kids these days. While strict parenting does produce better behaved children, too many times I've seen it produce a kid who has low self-esteem, a lack of social skills, and in the long run, more problems. Or I see a parent's intent to raise a moralistic child backfire and create a child who spins out of control. I suggest a different approach.

That approach includes setting clear boundaries and allowing these boundaries to speak for you so that you don't have to be so strict. Limiting, restricting, preventing, withholding, protecting, and restraint are all needed in raising kids. I suggest that parents do those things less and allow their kids to be exposed to more during the time they're under a parent's influence, to speak truth to children when they're exposed to error, and to be a strong voice of reason and wisdom as a child pursues owning his or her faith and fleshing out how that faith fits in today's culture. Remember that the forbidden fruit tastes the sweetest, and many times a parent's well-intended withholding makes a child want to taste that fruit all the more.

Effective Techniques for Parenting Teens

Because I live with sixty kids on our Heartlight campus and parent them in the absence of their parents, I have to find what is effective for the teenagers who live with us. I've found that setting clear boundaries, developing rules that uphold what I believe, administering agreed-upon consequences for inappropriate behavior, and then allowing kids the freedom to make choices within the boundaries, provides an opportunity for me to back down on the strictness and focus more on the relationship. This model gives teens freedom, the ability to make choices, and control of their life to some degree, and it forces them to assume responsibility for their life. It also takes me out of the role of authoritarian and into a role of relationship. As I've said many times, kids change because of relationship, not authority.

If there's just a hint of questioning of your ability, a trace of concern that your child isn't headed on the path you want, or there's a smidgeon of concern that the culture is a little bit overwhelming and perhaps irresistible for your teen or tween, then please consider this chapter carefully.

As children move into the teenage years, parents many times feel somewhat overwhelmed by the number of activities and privileges there are to be given to a child. They may even feel somewhat of a target when a child comes home and expresses "Everyone else gets to do this!" "You're so lame, Mom . . . Why can't I do this?" "Why are you so strict?" or "Dad, everyone else has this; why can't I?" Ever heard these before? My suggestion is that you outline an age-appropriate list of privileges, possessions, and possibilities for your child and determine *what* will be appropriate *when*.

How do you know what is age appropriate? Talk to other trusted parents to find out what they allow and have some discussion about what's appropriate. What's appropriate in east Texas may not necessarily be appropriate in southern California. And what's good at one age in one social circle isn't always so good in another.

Someone asked me at a parenting seminar what would be a good age for a child to get a cell phone. I chuckled at the question, as this topic is an age-shifting privilege. Who would have ever thought that a junior high kid would one day ever carry a phone that could reach around the world in their pocket? Just a few years ago, it was unheard of for a senior high student to have a phone. I talked with a family who allowed their fifth grader to have a phone, and I chatted with a ninety-five-year-old man at the airport who got a cell phone three years ago. So here's my answer: somewhere between ten and ninety-two years old is the best time to give your child a phone.

See why it's important to know what other parents of kids in your child's peer group are doing?

Privileges and Expectations

Here are some areas of privileges and beliefs that are the most asked-about topics at my speaking engagements. I bet you can come up with other items that need to be tackled in your home. After listing all those areas that you think need addressing, go through each one and determine a timeline that would let your child know year-by-year expectations for them that show them how you desire to move them to independence and allow them to make more and more choices about their life as they get older. This is not an exhaustive list:

- Cell phone usage and texting
- Church attendance
- Curfew on weekdays and weeknights
- Dating or courting
- Dress and appearance
- Driving a car
- Extracurricular activities
- Facebook activity
- Going to the mall
- Doing homework
- Internet access
- Involvement in activities
- Movies to watch
- Music
- Rewards for positive behavior
- Sleepovers
- Employment

Let me address a couple of these and show you a couple of examples of how I would time-line these items and communicate them to your kids.

Church Attendance

- When you're twelve and thirteen, you'll need to attend church and Sunday school with your family and go to youth group every Wednesday night.
- When you're fourteen and fifteen, you can go to either the Saturday night or Sunday service for church, attend Sunday school, and go to youth group on Wednesday nights.
- When you're sixteen, you can drive to church service on Saturday or Sunday night, and we won't require you to attend youth group on Wednesday nights.
- When you're seventeen, you can choose whether to go to church or to go to youth group on Sunday nights.
- When you're eighteen, you're more than welcome to go to church with us if you want to.

See the progression? Don't focus on what you are giving up. Rather, focus on what your child has the opportunity to choose. You are letting them make more and more decisions as they age, which gives them the feeling that they're in control of their life and empowers them to make decisions.

When they're seventeen years old and come downstairs on Sunday morning and say, "I don't want to go to church today," don't shame them or make them feel second-class for not choosing what you want. Instead, let them know, "Sure . . . why don't you meet us for lunch so we can spend some time together?" You must give your older teens the opportunity to exercise their freedom to choose and trust what you have taught them about the need for spiritual nourishment. Here's another one.

Facebook Activity

- When you're twelve, you won't be able to have a Facebook page.
- When you're thirteen and fourteen, you can have a page and can only check it once a day for thirty minutes. And you must "friend" both Mom and Dad, and we'll be watching your and others' entries until you're fifteen. We will approve pictures before you post.
- When you're fifteen, you can spend one hour a day on Facebook as long as it doesn't take away from family time, completing your homework, or keeping you up so late that you can't get up on your own in the morning. We're still watching!
- When you're sixteen, no more than two hours on Facebook and make sure that your language is appropriate.
- When you're seventeen, it's all yours.
- When you're eighteen, I hope that you'll accept my "friend" request.

Again, notice the progression. Here's another one.

Cell Phone and Texting

- When you're twelve, you can use my cell phone in the afternoons when I'm not using it.

- When you're thirteen, we'll get you a cell phone and you can text no more than forty times a day and we're going to be checking all your texts.
- When you're fourteen, you can text no more than sixty texts a day, and we'll still be watching. And if you ever send an inappropriate picture, we'll limit your texting. Just texting, no sexting.
- When you're fifteen, you can text all you want as long as it doesn't interfere with homework, sleep, communication, and relationships. We're still going to stalk your phone.
- When you're sixteen, we'll buy you a cell phone, but you will have to pay for half the bill every month.
- When you're seventeen, you pay for your phone. It's now your responsibility. Text as much as you want.
- When you're eighteen, will you call us occasionally? Or text?

A mother told me recently that her daughter takes her cell phone to bed and texts to her friends all through the night until she falls asleep. She stated that they've had fights over when the phone needs to be turned off. She said her daughter is sixteen. My questions to her and her responses are listed here.

Does your daughter get up on her own and get herself ready for school? Yes.

Does she do well in school? Yes.

Does she talk to you when she gets home from school? Yes.

Does she do all her homework? Yes.

Is she respectful of family members and engages well with everyone? Yes.

Then, what's the problem? (Silence.)

Do I want a child taking a cell phone to bed? No. Do I think a

sixteen-year-old needs to text all night long? No. Would I ever rec-
ommend that someone answer the phone every time it rings? No.
Is it necessary to remain connected with others while one sleeps?
No. But if it's *not causing* a problem, why *make* it a problem? In my
neck of the woods we would say there are "bigger fish to fry."

A Strategy for Privileges That Works

Moms and dads, there is a sweet spot between strictness and permissiveness, and it is far better to fault on the side of the latter than
the former. It's important to find that spot where your child feels a
little restrained and longs for the next step, instead of feeling that
there's no hope of getting more privileges in life, so he just gives up
and doesn't care.

When trying to figure out the schedule of what privileges to
give when, I would encourage you to consider this. I've come to
the conclusion that many parents could avoid a lot of drama if
they would just give what their kids will eventually get anyway,
just a bit sooner. If you think your child should get a cell phone
at age thirteen, give it to her at twelve and a half. If you don't
think he should date until age sixteen, let him start at fifteen and
a half. Giving privileges to your kids a few months early maintains
a relationship that could be destroyed if they have to rebel for their
freedom. Look, you're eventually going to give the privilege to
them anyway. So give the privilege, build some agreed parameters
around it, and take it away should they fail to hold up their end of
the agreement.

Next, set the rules for your home for behaviors (and probable
behaviors) that are particular to your home for your situation and

for the specific issues you're dealing with. Limit your long list of rules to the ten most important for your family. These need to be determined by age, your history with a particular child, what you believe, and what values you determine are important for your family.

Here's my list of ten things that I think are important enough to develop rules around, letting all know what the family policy is on these particular items and what the consequence will be for violating a family rule.

1. Bullying
2. Disrespect
3. Dishonesty
4. Drugs/alcohol
5. Disobedience
6. Failing classes
7. Inappropriate Internet activity
8. Sexual activity
9. Texting while driving (then parents better not do this either!)
10. Deceitfulness and lying

Next, determine the consequences for breaking the rules. This is basically a system that says, "You do the crime, you do the time." And don't rescue your child from the consequences. The value of determining boundaries within your family, and then setting rules and consequences, is to let this model be the authority where you don't have to parent with strictness. Once this system is in place, then you will have the opportunity to develop deeper relationships with your kids. Just make sure you are enforcing the consequences of a child's chosen behavior. Don't rescue them from consequences; you'll only have to rescue them again when they violate the rule a second time.

So what consequences do you set? To formulate what consequence goes with each rule, determine what your child likes doing the most, and take that away when they violate the most important rule that you have established.

For example, if you think that respect is the most important rule in your home, and your child loves texting on the cell phone more than anything else, then link those two together and make a rule and consequence that might look like this: "If you are disrespectful to anyone in the family, you will lose your cell phone for one week. When there is a second offense, make it three weeks. And if disrespect happens a third time, the cell phone is gone."

Once the rules and consequences are agreed upon, then allow the system to work. It's saying to your child, "Here's the list of privileges, and here are the agreed-upon rules." You let these boundaries determine the parameters and give your child the freedom to act within the rules that have been placed around him. Let the system work.

And loosen up a little. Give your child something you've withheld for quite some time. It will show her that you are for her, not against her. Surprise your child, and she might just surprise you with her response.

Add boundaries, subtract strictness, and it equals opportunities for growth.

>>> 15 <<<

See Conflict as a
Precursor to Change

Timing is everything when confronting the conflict that inevitably happens within any home. The effectiveness of the resolution of conflict will determine the type of relationship you have with your child and will give you opportunities to dive deeper into the life of your child, more than any chance you have to affect their teenage years. Resolving conflict can usher in a new day of hope if done correctly, or it can damage your family in such a way that sometimes takes a lifetime to recover. Timing is everything.

When John and Michelle brought their son, Dirk, to see me, all three were angry. They were furious that they had to meet with someone to help them resolve their conflicts. The first time we met lasted a couple of hours: I wanted to find out why their heap of unresolved conflict was so big and what was driving the comments that I kept hearing throughout the discussion. Their conversations were filled with unforgiving comments such as "you never," "you always," "well, you should," and "right!" coupled with hurtful comments like "I can't stand you," "you'll never get it," "just forget it," "I'd rather not talk about it," and "I never said that."

Their heap was deep! It wasn't a pile of huge problems, but

it was full of a lot of little unresolved things that had piled up over time and had started to spill over into their relationships. Unresolved issues always have a way of coming back around, and it was damaging this family.

Dirk was a good kid, and the conflict that he was causing was what I would consider minor and normal adolescent issues: girlfriends, not wanting to do homework, occasionally staying out too late, a curse word at an inappropriate time, breaking some of Mom's fine china (unintentionally), not putting tools back where they belong, carving his girlfriend's name in the front yard with the lawnmower, skipping out of swim practice, getting a speeding ticket, an occasional bending of the truth, listening to music his parents disapproved of, wearing his pants too low, getting a small tattoo without permission, texting too much, watching an occasional movie that wasn't supposed to be watched, and viewing some inappropriate websites. These are just all normal issues that most families deal with. It was the way that this family was dealing with conflict that caused the problem.

John, the dad, didn't discuss the little issues that came up until the heap was big enough for all to see and he had to address it. His pent-up anger would usually explode like a volcano spewing relational hurt over all the family and burn up any hope of anyone thinking that he was an approachable man. His timing was off.

Michelle, the mom, couldn't leave well enough alone and nit-picked and nagged about every little issue that came up, which only made John (the dad) even angrier and pushed Dirk to turn off his mother's comments. She just didn't feel like she could go to bed at night without resolving anything she thought was wrong, for fear they'd miss the opportunity to teach Dirk a lesson. Her timing was off.

Between Dad's occasional explosions and Mom's constant nagging, Dirk did neither, and he bottled up all his emotions, hurts, and feelings. I think the three of them had come to the conclusion that they needed to sort out what was going on before their conflict got out of hand. Who was at fault the most? They all were. And it was going to be a concerted effort to get them back on track.

Using Conflict to Create Deeper Relationships

This situation is not unlike that of many families I come across in my travels, those who attend conferences we have at my home, or those families who place kids with us to live for a year. And I tell all parents that conflict can open the door to deeper relationships with their kids, but only when the timing is right.

Dads, it's not okay to bottle up and delay or postpone dealing with the conflict that happens in your home. And it's never okay to just ignore it, hoping that it will go away.

When the dashboard warning light of anger flashes on your control panel, it is a signal to you that something is wrong. You must overcome your fear of conflict wherever that fear comes from and understand that your role is to counter the negative influences in your child's life. That warning light comes on when you think or say any of the following:

- "I'm not comfortable about that."
- "I don't like the situation."
- "I don't feel good about my child's involvement in this."
- "I can't support this activity."

- "This makes me mad when he does this."
- "We need to think of a different course of action."
- "There's got to be an alternative."
- "This isn't good."
- "This isn't going to happen."
- "Is this what she really wants?"

To ignore the potential for conflict and to disengage from your child when these lights come on only allows for future behaviors, habits, and pathways to be reckoned with at a later time. Avoid issues now, and they will come later when they are much bigger, whose consequences are usually much greater.

To embrace the conflict ushers in a world of change that has the possibility of keeping your child from having to walk a path he or she really never wants to be on. Confronting minor issues now saves you the energy of having to deal with bigger issues later.

Moms, while your intent in dealing with everything your child does wrong is good, the intensity of addressing every single issue every day has a mighty way of shutting your child down, just like it did Dirk. Your timing is off. As I stated earlier in this book, people change because of relationship, not the exertion of authority in the form of nagging and badgering, even when it's done in the right spirit to help, or because something is not right. If you correct everything, there will be no time left to develop that relationship.

Conflict will come in your years of raising your teens, as sure as the changing seasons. I encourage parents to look at conflict as an opportunity to speak directly to the issues or struggles in the life of your child. The presence of conflict gives you a new way of teaching that provides an excellent window of opportunity to help your children assimilate what they know and make personal application into their conflicted world. Grip it as an opportunity to usher in change to their life. This is the upbringing you have been called to. It's the teaching your child so desperately needs and, to many parents' surprise, so desperately wants. But your timing must be spot-on. Because if not, you'll miss this wonderful opportunity.

Schedule a Time to Work through Conflict

Let me address the issue of timing by asking you a question. Do you have the equivalent of one work week to spend with your child to change the nature of your relationship that resolves conflict? If you do, then I'm going to ask you to give that time in one-hour segments where you get with your child, away from home, to talk about conflict and commit yourself to its resolution. In chapter 10, I asked you to spend a meal together with your child just to ask questions. This request is just a little different. The purpose is to resolve conflict.

Call it your "Confrontation over Coffee" time, your "Coke and Conflict" time, or your "Disagreements during Donuts" time, but find a time to sit down and let your child know, no matter what age they are, that this is the place, the opportunity, and the time, to resolve any issues that arise. I always like having these types of talks in a public setting as I'm not walking on anyone's turf, and the others present has a way of keeping emotions in check should they begin to inflate. (For ideas about how to start discussions about conflict resolution, see appendix B.)

Why once a week? Because it acts as a release valve to prevent pressure from building up and blowing up like a volcano, or keeps the constancy of everyday correction to vent just like a slow-release pressure valve that will regulate the size of the heap, and keep relationships happening. And if a week is too short of a time span to meet, make it every other week. But keep it regular.

The High Cost of Unresolved Conflict

What most people don't realize is that there is a great cost to unresolved conflict. All the time spent in the presence of unresolved conflict when relationships come to a standstill, is time that could have been spent building a deeper relationship and helping your child make the changes they need in their teen years.

Moms and dads, speak to the obvious elephant in the room. "Dumbo" is there for a reason. It is at these points of contact that you have an opportunity to show your child how their faith intersects their reasoning capability. This is not the time for Dad to decide to go mow the yard or get busy in the garage fixing something. And it's not a time for Mom to deliver her well-rehearsed five-point sermon. It's a time to engage with your child to offer help and direction in the midst of the conflict, either with you, your rules, or with an aspect of his world. Unresolved conflict doesn't go away—it will only reappear later. If parents avoid conflict at all costs and pretend like everything is great, nothing will change. Connection will be lost and each family member will eventually drift apart, just like John and Michelle and their son, Dirk.

I've been counseling teens for years, and I always have to remind myself, *These are teens. There's going to be conflict. I'm here to help them grow deeper in their understanding. Our relationship must remain intact even if I get angered over not getting what I want for them.* I must enter the conflict with the teen by understanding that conflict is a precursor to change, and my focus must be on not what has happened but what will come out of our resolution.

Second, I must remember that the goal of conflict resolution must be about the person I'm having the conflict with. It's not about *me being right.* It's not about my disappointment. It's not about the effect one's mistake has made on me. It's not about me feeling like a failure of a parent. It isn't about me; it's about the teenager. The goal of entering into conflict has got to be the mind-set that the one I am resolving issues with right now is the most important person in the room.

And third, I want to speak the truth in love. Not yelling, screaming, complaining, berating—just speaking. And my words need to be the truth, not speculation, what others might think, or my feelings that can't be substantiated. I must speak the truth. It's also got to be spoken in love—not hatred, disgust, frustration, or rage. If I can't speak to the conflict with a teenager in love, then I need to take a breather and cool off before engaging. If not, the conflict will appear to be more about me than about the teen, which shifts the focus off where the change really needs to happen. Have you ever gotten into a discussion when you tried to confront someone, and quickly the tables turn and now its all about you? This is what I want to keep from happening.

The process of dealing with conflict gets easier over time. But I don't think it gets any more comfortable no matter how many times you're involved in conflict resolution. I believe it gets easier because you start to see the bigger picture of conflict, but it doesn't get any more comfortable. I've just learned that it's okay not to be comfortable, and not to let my discomfort keep me from doing what is right.

I haven't met a teen yet who doesn't want to change. Little do they know that the majority of their change in their teenage years will happen as a result of conflict and by doing things they don't really want to do; like resolving, forgiving, forgetting, learning the hard way, and listening to truth.

Don't Run from Conflict

Don't run from conflict when it arises with your child. It's an opportunity that will benefit them greatly.

I hate going to the dentist. But I love my dentist, Krista, dearly. I hate getting shots to numb my mouth (there's never a right time, in my view). But I get them because I wouldn't want to have her work on my mouth without them. My blood pressure rises when I sit in her dentist chair, and I begin to sweat when she enters the room; I know what's going to happen. I white-knuckle that chair the whole time as my legs shake to dispel my nervous energy. While she's working, I try to think of distant happy places, with happy thoughts, and pray for comfort as I wish I was somewhere else. But I love my dentist.

The experience of confronting teens and entering into conflict is about as much fun as going to the dentist. But there are some important lessons to learn about my visits to my dentist. Here they are. Krista's desire is to help me. When I'm in the chair, it's all about me, not about her. She tries to numb the pain as best she can. She understands my fear (some would call it wimpyness). She stays on task until the job is complete. We hug when it's all over, and my teeth and I are better for it. The relationship with her is even better. And any time I have a problem with my teeth, I call her quickly and she helps me again. I love my dentist not only for who she is but for what she does for me. See the similarities?

The resolution of conflict before it gets out of hand changes people in three ways. The first change is with your child. The second change is you. And the third, most important change is your relationship with your child. Your willingness to enter conflict with your child sends a clear message that you are willing to risk the relationship for their betterment and communicates to them, "I can love you when you are doing well and have it all together, and I can love you equally as well when you're struggling and maybe falling apart."

The resolution of conflict is all about timing. Adolescence is the time that conflict will happen because it is the time you're wanting them to apply what you've taught as they experiment, explore, and find explanation. So use the natural conflicts that arise during these years as opportunities to go deeper in your relationship with them.

It's all about timing.

Pick Your Battles Wisely

While conflict can be healthy and promote growth, *constant* conflict can drown relationships. Parents who engage in a battle over every little thing they disagree with in their teen's life—from unmade beds to a poor test grade—will find that the only change they get from their teen is an increase in the tides of resentment washing over every member of the family. It's essential to the life of the family and the sanity of each member for parents to identify the important battles that need to be fought and leave the less important ones to take care of themselves. This assists parents in determining where their personal battle lines need to be drawn, so that they are fighting for the important issues. It helps parents create teachable moments with their teens so that growth can occur. It also shows parents how to keep the goal of maturity and healthy adulthood in the forefront, so they can decide which issues should be fought for and which will not matter in the long run.

When I was a senior in high school, my favorite teacher, John Roberts, asked me a question that got me thinking. I still think about the question often and catch myself evaluating my life by determining how to implement the answers that surface in my mind. The question asked years ago was this: "If your house was on fire and you could only take three things from that house, what would you take?" Remember when I said earlier that learning the art of asking questions could keep your teen thinking for years? Well, this teacher did a wonderful job of asking questions that shifted my "thinker" from neutral to drive throughout my senior year.

I think my answer back then was my guitar, my swimming trophies, and a ring that my high school sweetheart (who later became my wife) had given me the year before. My choices showed a little immaturity and a whole lot of self-centeredness. As I think back to these things, I wonder why I didn't mention things like my dog, my sister, my parents, family treasures, cash, and so on. It wasn't that these things weren't important, I just thought, in my limited thinking capability, that the others were *more* important.

I found out quickly how important those "things" really were when I returned home from college at Oklahoma State University. One week after my return, a number of tornados ripped through Tulsa, Oklahoma, and blew away my concept of what was important. I lost my guitar, my trophies, and that precious ring when we lost the whole house. That tragedy rocked my world and forced me to make some life-changing decisions, based upon my newly formed concepts of what was really important. I left Oklahoma State University and moved to Tulsa University, asked my high school sweetheart to marry me (she said yes), and decided I was going to start working with kids. Amazing what a little wind, a little storm, a dark cloud, and the questioning of what is important can do to one's life.

What Are Your "Five Things"?

Let me rephrase the question that was asked of me and ask you one that would help you line out what is important in your home. *If you had to limit confrontation of issues at your home to just five things,* *what would those five areas of confrontation be?* Pick your battles wisely, you only have five.

Would it be a scuffle to limit or restrict the music they listen to? Would it be a melee over their hair—how they wear it, what color it is, the length, or them shaving their head? Would it be the battle over going to church or choosing which church to go to? Would there be a war over their academics and grades and performance, or would it be the types of peers they want to hang out with? Would it be a skirmish over the amount of time they spend playing video games or disputes over how much time a teen needs to spend online?

Would there be a conflict over your definition and their definition of modesty? Whether your daughter is showing too much cleavage or your son has his pants hanging halfway down his rear end? Would you choose to have encounters about the kids having tattoos and getting piercings or would there be arguments over the type of makeup your kids will wear? Could there be fracases over Facebook language, whether it is what your child writes or the wording and comments of some of their friends' posts? Would you struggle over the use of words that suddenly seem more present and appropriate than words of yesteryear?

Would there be frays about relationships you've cautioned your child to remain distant from? Would you fight over the issues of disobedience, disrespect, and dishonesty? Or would you put up your dukes over the types of movies your child watches? Would it be worth dueling over whether your child could be sexually active or challenge a child's desire to use alcohol and drugs? Would there be a kerfuffle when a child doesn't keep their room tidy and clean? Would there be controversies over a child drinking and driving, or clashes over your child texting while driving?

That is a long list of battles to fight, isn't it? And I'm sure you could add a few more of your own battles to the list. If you try to correct or manage all of the things on the list, you'll spend most of your time fighting and possibly destroying your relationship with your child in the process. There are way too many things to fight over, all with great cause and support. To try to conquer all is a purposeful crusade that might look good on paper, but fleshing it out might look terrible in the life of your child.

Let me tell you why I think this topic of picking your battles wisely is so important. I believe that kids are overwhelmed in a culture that bombards them with information, new lifestyles, new challenges, and new pressures to perform and appear certain ways. That increased pressure is moving our teens from normal teenage angst (apprehension or insecurity) to increasing levels of anxiety (an overwhelming uneasiness and apprehension about future uncertainties) and depression. The symptoms of clinical depression, which are always to be taken seriously, might include a loss of pleasure or interest in something a teen once did or loved, a feeling of extremely low self-esteem, a sense of guilt that they can't get it together, mood swings, decreased or increased longing for either sleep or food, an inability to focus, or zapped energy levels that destroy motivation.

The last thing any parent wants to do is to push his or her child beyond the normal limits of teenage angst, in the name of integrity, principle, and high standards, only to find out through some tragedy or storm blowing through their neck of the woods what is really important.

Pick Your Battles

Parents, pick your battles with your child and don't try to fight them all at once. Your child is already coming home battle weary from the challenges presented by the culture they are living in, so to add more battle tours to their already full schedule might give them a push that a parent never intended. Don't overload your child with an endless list of things to do, things to change, corrections galore, and ways to improve what they're already struggling to prove. Check your overloading, and be careful to not overwhelm your child, as it may move them to exasperation and anger. Then you'll have a whole lot more battles to fight.

Do I feel that the battles I've listed are unimportant? No! It's just that I believe in many situations there are battles that can wait to be fought, there are some that can be lost that won't change the bigger picture effort of the war, and there are some that are worth dying for. As I mentioned earlier, the question I ask parents frequently is, "Are you willing to die on that hill?" When they share various impasses they're having with a child when it comes to privileges, rules, boundaries, and correctional comments I want them to think through their battle plan.

I'm not saying that those issues you are fighting for are not important. I am saying that there might be some *more* important battles to fight and that in the small skirmishes in which you're engaging, you might be missing the bigger challenges that need your effort.

Here are the questions that I would ask you:

- Out of all the hills out there on the landscape of
  adolescence, which ones are you willing to die on?

- What issues can be allowed to simmer on the back burner, while you move that which needs to be cooked to the front burner?
- What are the major issues, and what are the minor issues?
- What's important and what's not?
- What will die out on its own, and what demands your attention?
- What needs to be learned now, and what can be learned later?
- What's eternal, and what's temporal?

Some people used to think that boys having long hair was a hill to die on. Some thought that tattoos were a mark of evil or indicative of a thug. Some parents used to believe that a shaved head was a sign of a redneck racist. Some parents considered ear piercings on guys to be a question of sexuality. Some thought that heavy makeup and teased hair were marks of a girl parents hoped their son would never bring home. People used to think that the earth was flat. Sounds kind of ridiculous now, doesn't it? I wonder what views and positions we have today that will one day be considered the same. If there are some, I encourage you to look at and let go of those views before you damage your relationship with your child.

Which Hills Will You Die On?

It's a valuable exercise to ask yourself some questions about the hills on which you're going to do battle as you decide what is important for your kids. In choosing your five issues, I ask you to consider your answers to the following thought provokers.

What issues have the greatest consequences? If you have only five areas to choose, which will affect your child the most should they win in their battle to get what they want? Is your daughter's hair color really more important than whether she's having sex with her boyfriend? If you had to choose between the music your son listens to and addressing the issue of texting while driving, which might save his life?

What battles, if you lose, will also cause you to lose a relationship with your child? If you choose to die on the particular hill of Facebook entries by taking away Facebook privileges, are you willing to win that war and create a bigger war when your child chooses to socialize in other ways? Is your desire to withhold the privilege of a cell phone, when all your kid's friends have one, worth having your child think that you're old-fashioned, too strict, and working against him when he's going to need you the most in the days ahead?

What battles will eventually pass? In a recent study, the *Journal of Psychology Research* shows children ages nine to eleven now hold "fame" as their number-one value (it ranked fifteenth in a list of values in 1997).[1] I think this is a pretty normal response to a celebrity-crazed world where everybody's got talent, they all want to be an idol, and YouTube stardom is just a click away. The efforts to try to change your child's mind about her desire or belief that she will be a celebrity or star is wasted breath. So use your breath on something that is important, not something that she'll learn eventually anyway.

What is the emotional condition of your child? If your adolescent is battle-weary, sometimes it is best to back off completely for a while. Timing is everything. Too much at any time can tip the scales of emotional balance toward anxiety and depression. It's important for you to know the stability of your child. The day to confront your daughter about how she's treating everyone in the family would not be a good thing if her boyfriend just broke up with her that day.

What's essential and what's not? In other words, what really matters? I've heard parents tell me that the reason they make their child clean their room and keep it organized and free of clutter, dirty clothes, and empty soda cans is because "cleanliness is next to godliness," "a tidy room makes for a tidy mind," or "a clean room is a happy room." The number of relationships between parent and teens that I've seen destroyed because of this one issue saddens me, perhaps because I almost ruined my relationship with my son over his slob lifestyle that I interpreted as a show of disrespect for property and my meticulous and obsessive tendencies to have everything clean and in its place.

When my son was in the tenth grade I worried about him having a dirty room. But as I thought about it, I realized that I had never met a kid who had died of a dirty room. But I will tell you that I know of a young man who committed suicide who once told me that "the only thing my mom cares about is the cleanliness of my room." Amazing, a dirty room doesn't bother me anymore.

That's not the way that I want to learn what is important. I've had one tornado in my life . . . I don't want another.

>>> 17 <<<

Love When You Don't Feel Like It

Alex was a pretty good kid who had an amazing ability to make people laugh. His wittiness was charming, his humor was funny, and he got along with other kids well. He had lived with us a few months and I wondered when we were going to see the reasons his parents sent him to us. We saw them one afternoon when he arrived home from school—and what wasn't present was his smile that we had all grown so used to.

Upon getting out of the van that drives them back and forth from school, Alex walked intensely to a storage shed where we stored all the athletic equipment, picked up a baseball bat, and proceeded to beat the van until there were huge craters and dents totaling about twenty-five hundred dollars' worth of damage, all the while yelling, "I'm tired of riding in this van!" As I walked up to him, my golden retriever, Copper, was also walking up to me. In a split second, Alex drop-kicked Copper in the dog's gut, causing Copper to yelp and scream in pain. I thought he had just killed my dog. I ran over to Copper, who was now lying down, and one of the other kids ran up to help and made a comment that still rings in my ears. He said, "Hard to love a kid like that, isn't it?"

Of course, my response was that I was angry with Alex. By the time I took care of Copper and one of our other staff took care of Alex and calmed him down, I was seething mad that some kid had just kicked my dog. I tell you, I was hot. There was nothing godly about my thoughts as I felt this kid had violated everything about me, my dog, my property, our relationship, my trust with him, and my confidence in his heart. It took me three days to cool off enough to talk to him.

During my cooling-off period, I thought about what I have told so many parents: the behavior you see is just a symptom of something else going on in your child's life. There was something else going on (there always is). The divorce between his mom and dad was killing him. And the fact that his dad had just been convicted of child molestation was tearing him apart. The van and my dog were just victims of this kid's anger.

The first time I saw Alex after the incident, I wanted to tell him how he caused quite a bit of damage to an animal that did nothing but a bunch of tail waggin' and begging for someone to throw a ball. I wanted to tell him that he would have to pay for the damage he caused to the van, and getting to school was going to look a little different for the next few days. I wanted him to pay. I wanted him to feel bad about what he had done. I wanted to chew him out and put him in his place.

But that wasn't what he needed. At that moment, Alex needed to feel like someone cared about him not only when he was doing well but also when he had really messed up.

As I walked up to him, I realized that what I wanted and what he needed were two different things. His eyes looked down in shame, and in a split second, I knew this young man needed to feel that he was loved. I opened my arms and wrapped them around him, told him that our relationship was good, that I understood his frustration, and asked if he wanted to go with me to see Copper, who was recuperating at the vet. We stopped at a nearby coffee shop and talked about the incident. I consoled him about his dad and helped him figure out how he was going to pay for the vet bill and the damage to the van. After a few days, I told him that the bill for the van had been forgiven, but he still had to pay for the vet.

In my heart of hearts, I still wanted him to be shamed for what he had done. I wanted him to feel every ounce of anger that I had felt toward him. But I knew that this wasn't going to benefit anyone, so I decided to pay for the van and let it go. He still had consequences for his actions and had to pay for a hefty vet bill, but more importantly, he felt loved when he had screwed up. It was a lesson I would gladly pay twenty-five hundred dollars for a child to learn any day.

My choice was to love him when he didn't deserve it. In my world, that's called grace: getting something when you don't deserve it.

Don't Give Up

In more than three decades of living and working with kids, I've learned that if I walk away from the relationship every time someone offends me, then I allow their actions to determine the type of relationship I really want with them. I've been disappointed a lot. I've been offended many times by many kids. I've been disrespected, disobeyed, and have had many who have been dishonest with me. I've been taken advantage of, stolen from, and ridiculed. And while it hurts every time I feel the sting from their lack of consideration, I know that if I quit and give up, the relationship stops, and the hope for anything in the future becomes dim.

To love someone when you have been wronged is tough, but it's essential in communicating a love that is beyond your capability. It's a love that will win out if you don't quit. Even if you don't feel like it.

For me, it's called grace. It's moving relationally toward a person when they have wronged you. It's opening the door of your heart when every part of you wants to shut it off. It's engaging when you have every right to disengage. It's offering help when someone's actions have violated everything you believe in, hope for, and want for that person. It's staying involved in the relationship when someone has violated your rules, ignored your advice, or hurt you through lies, deceit, and manipulation.

When you feel good about giving grace, it probably isn't grace.

What Grace Looks Like in a Family

Here are some examples of what grace may look like with your child when your feelings are telling you otherwise:

- It's taking your child out to dinner when he's grounded for stealing money out of your purse.
- It's taking your daughter away for a couple of days to spend some quality time with her after you find out she's been having sex with her boyfriend.
- It's going up to your drama queen's room and sitting down and talking to her a few minutes after she blew up at your wife and used some words that you'll never find in Scripture.

- It's hugging your son and telling him, "We're going to get through this," after he tells you that his girlfriend is pregnant.
- It's not saying what you want to say (and have every reason to), and saying what needs to be heard when your tough guy just got expelled from school from defending the honor of his sister . . . the wrong way.
- It's taking your son to sit down for a man-to-man talk instead of wanting to poke his eyes out after your wife finds him looking at pornography on the Internet.
- It's not saying anything when a lot could be said, thus allowing the feelings of wrongdoing that need to be felt the opportunity to teach a lesson that your words could never achieve.

Your movement toward your children when they make mistakes, choose poorly, encounter problems, or violate your standards lets them know that the issues have more to do with them than they do with you. Your actions by remaining engaged help them keep focused on their responsibility for what they have done or what they will need to do. And it keeps you in the relational position of being one who wants to help them through their difficulties, rather than one who is to assume responsibility to "fix" what has happened, solve the issue, or exert your authority.

It's a movement toward them when every part of you is crying out, "Walk away." It's tough, but well worth it in the long run of adolescence. It moves you from the authoritative directive style of their preteen years into a relational instructor mentality that sends a message that you will never leave them, you are for them, and you will be with them whatever they encounter in life. Talk about some teachable moments!

Please understand this. You can relate with your children well, ask a million questions, stop controlling everything in their life, help them become independent, quit being so strict, learn that conflict is good as you pick your battles wisely, and spend all the time in the world with them. But if you retract your relationship when they mess up, you invalidate all you've been building, and all your good intentions of loving your child through their adolescent years will go down the drain.

Now don't get me wrong on this point. I also believe in mercy: not getting the negative consequences that you deserve. But not to the point of rescue, where a child wiggles her way out of consequences with a silver tongue, cuteness, or a display of tears. And I believe in grace: getting a positive reward that you don't deserve. But not to the point of enabling a child or giving him license to continue with the same behaviors. Parents should line out rules in such a way that consequences push a child away from inappropriate behaviors and the relationship pulls them toward the path that parents want their child to walk.

Grace and Love Trump Rebellion and Pain

Meet Bri. She came to my residential treatment center, and nothing I did seemed to get through to this rebellious kid. She continuously neglected what was required from her. She not only offended me by her actions, but also she intentionally disregarded boundaries, broke rules, and cared little about the consequences. I've never met an angrier child and have never been more frustrated with a kid. During one of our intense conversations I asked her, "What do you want from me?"

With head hung low, Bri responded, "Love me when I least deserve it, 'cause that's when I need it the most." Bri's answer stopped me dead in my tracks. As I hugged her, I kept thinking, *What she needs is grace.* Bri needed to be loved when she didn't deserve it . . . loved when I felt anything but loving toward her.

We all want love and acceptance, especially when are acting our worst. We know we're being bad, and we want to be loved anyway. I believe teens want this more than anything.

Grace and love trump punishment and pain. Parents do not need to move away from appropriate consequences or to lower their standards and accept bad behavior and broken rules. But they do need to love and accept their child right where he is, especially when he's at his worst.

Grace does not move away from accountability, but it always moves to embrace the offender.

>>> 18 <<<

Offer Freedom to Make Mistakes

M ark Twain once said, "There are no mistakes in life; there are only lessons to be learned." Just as parents delay the maturation process when they do not hand over some control to their kids, they also can cause their children harm if they don't create a family atmosphere that allows for mistakes; because mistakes are inevitable when adolescents begin making decisions.

You can avoid your child making mistakes in any of the following ways:

- Don't let them do anything or participate with anyone in any activity.
- Do everything for them so they never have opportunity to make a decision.
- Don't teach about making decisions in their life.

Any of these three scenarios is a crisis waiting to happen. Many parents have seemingly perfect kids because they've never been given the chance to make decisions. These parents think all is going well with their parenting style, and to their dismay, they realize later that they were only postponing the inevitable (their child making mistakes) to a later time in life where consequences for mistakes are greater.

An example of this would be a child who was never taught about money and finances. As a result, the child never had to make decisions about spending, saving, stewardship, and accountability about financial matters. Looking at this child during his teen years, it would be easy to say that this child doesn't have any problem with finances, because he was never given the opportunity to handle money or finances. Fast-forward to the time that this now young adult is a newlywed and has to consider all of the above listed issues. While lessons can be learned as a newlywed, the postponement of the making mistakes now has potentially greater consequences. What's the number-one issue that newlyweds deal with their first year of marriage? Finances. According to Janice Hoffman, author of *Relationship Rules*, "The little things you overlooked when you were dating, you don't overlook them when you're married."[1] What appeared to be good parenting during the teen years, really wasn't that good, was it?

On the flip side, I've seen hundreds of kids who have made some colossal blunders in their teenage decision-making years. Yet learning life-changing lessons from these mistakes early on propelled these kids to maturity far beyond their years in contrast to the thousands of kids I have seen who were shielded from exercising their decision-making muscles during their teen years.

Give your child the opportunity to make mistakes, coupled with the freedom to make mistakes without the fear of shame, ridicule, or sarcasm. This gives your child permission to exercise their decision-making muscle so that they can carry the heavier loads of adulthood they will be required to lift.

The Parental Training Process—
Learn, Practice, Apply

With this in mind, the ideal parental training process is foundationally relational and is divided into three segments of a child's life: learning, practicing, and applying.

The first segment of life, from ages one to twelve, is all about a child *learning*. This is the time you pour into your child lessons, teachings, examples, models, principles, illustrations, instruction, directions, morals, values, and biblical standards through classes, church, discipline, activities, schooling, training, programs, and experiences. In this stage, *you teach your child everything you know to be true.*

The second segment of life occurs during a child's teen years, ages thirteen through nineteen. *Practicing* is the name of the game. Helping your child take what has been learned and develop decision-making muscle through exercise and rehearsal slowly exposes a child to the world in which they will live. In this stage, *you let your child practice what you have taught.*

The third segment of life is "the launch," where a child moves from adolescence to adulthood, ages twenty and above. In this stage, *you let your child apply what he or she knows to be true, tested, and relevant to the current culture.*

I would liken this to the simple progression of learning how to swim at an early age, and then swimming competitively for most of my teen years. I had a coach named Ben Simpson who would look at us before a swim competition and say, "You guys know what to do [learning], you've trained hard [practicing], now get in there and tear them up [applying]!" I suggest that parents say the same to their kids after plenty of training.

Give Kids Freedom to Make Mistakes

"Practice makes perfect" is an idiom that encourages the development of a skill through repetition coupled with positive feedback. Permission given to practice is important. Practice allows a child to develop the character quality of discernment, the ability to distinguish "what is good and bad for him" and choose the higher road.

A mother recently came up to me at one of our conferences and told me about her son. She said her son was active in their youth group at church, yet, "He sneaks around all the time, is deceitful, lies about where he is and what he is doing, sneaks out of the house, and is always mad at us. He tells us he does it because we don't let him do anything." When she answered my question of what it was that he wasn't allowed to do, I understood why her son was acting the way he was.

She continued, all in one sentence, "He's always been a good kid, but we won't allow him to have a cell phone until he's sixteen because he might text and drive but we're not going to let him use the car until he's eighteen because he's so immature and we don't let kids come to our house because his friends' parents allow them to date and they might bring their girls over and we don't allow him to, and we won't let him go over to his friends' houses because those parents don't have the same rules about music and movies that we do, and we don't believe in Facebook so he can't have an account there because there's so many predators and bad language and pictures he shouldn't be seeing, and we don't want him to make any mistakes."

With my eyes bulging and ears on overload, I said, "Wow, no wonder your son is acting the way he does. I would do the same." (She didn't like my answer.) I told her that she's got to trust what she has taught her son and trust God for his life. And my final words were, "You've got to lighten up and let your son fly, or you're going to lose him."

Under the banner of "overprotection" many parents isolate their kids, deny them the opportunity to fail, suppress their teens' desire to make decisions, beat down their spirit if they make a mistake, and withhold opportunities of learning that can turn good kids into disobedient kids.

I'm not saying that parents should irresponsibly expose our kids to everything and let the world teach them through the school of hard knocks with the mentality of "fend for yourself." We don't throw our children into the deep end of the pool and yell, "Swim!" to teach them to keep their head above water. We start in the shallow end and gradually let them go farther as they show that they can do better. Will they go under at times? Yes. Will they swallow water and choke? Yes. Will they go too far sometimes? Yes. I teach kids to swim this way because I know that they'll one day be in that deep end. I can always be on the watch . . . and I can jump in with them if they need my help. But I've got to let them learn to swim in their own pool. Practice, practice, practice.

Begin Transferring Responsibility to Your Child

When your tween begins turning into a teen, start flavoring your conversations with comments and questions that transfer you making decisions and placing that responsibility on them. You can say things like:

- "It's your choice."
- "Where do you want to go eat tonight?"

- "What do you want?"
- "You decide."
- "What do you think you ought to do?"
- "Not my decision."
- "Think it through, son."
- "I'll stand with you, but won't bail you out of this one."
- "You do what you feel best on this one, sweetheart."

I'm talking about helping a child make decisions at an early age where they learn to choose what they want to eat at McDonald's all the way up to choosing the college they'll attend and the person they'll marry. In between those two points are plenty of opportunities to exercise that decision-making muscle. Let them make as many decisions as possible.

Giving your kids the opportunity to make choices is one step in offering them the freedom to make mistakes. And your response to their mistakes is the second step that is equally vital to the atmosphere of practicing and flexing that decision-making muscle.

Respond to Mistakes with Gentleness and Grace

When your kids do make mistakes, shaming those mistakes can cause them to shut down, make them explosive in their response (shame upon shame), or worse, make them shut you out. Don't use comments like:

- "I told you so."
- "You should have listened."
- "Remember me saying that?"

- "I hope you learned your lesson."
- "Had to find out for yourself, didn't you?"

You don't have to shame them. They already know they made a mistake. The key when talking about that mistake is not to add shame or embarrass them more about something they're already embarrassed or shameful of. And if they don't feel that now, they will. Allow those consequences to have their full effect, and the guilt they've placed on themselves to teach them the lesson. Just remain quiet. You'll appear to be wise, your child will respect you for allowing him to learn a lesson from the mistake, and your relationship will remain intact. If you choose to make sure he's learned his lesson with words that just repeat why they should have listened, or with gestures that show disgust and disappointment, you will only push your kid away and never allow him the freedom to make a mistake.

Hopefully, in your gentle approach to their mistakes, you'll hear comments like:

- "You were right, Dad."
- "I should have listened, Mom."
- "I'll never do that again."
- "I know better."
- "I should have learned."
- "I had a feeling this was going to happen."
- "I know, I know. I won't happen again."
- "I messed up."

These are all comments that reveal that a child is learning. She's practicing what she's been taught because she was given the freedom to give it a try. This will give you some great conversations when you have your once-a-week meeting with your child.

>>> 19 <<<

Forgive When It's Hard

The example set by parents in the area of forgiveness is crucial to a child's development and is usually a character trait that is more caught than taught. If a parent holds a grudge when a child makes a mistake—big or small—the child learns that he is only worth loving when he does everything right. Ouch!

It's hard to forgive those who hurt you—even your kids—but forgiveness is vital for a family to stand strong against every storm. Forgiveness gives up hope that the past will ever change, but it keeps the faith that the future will be better and better. A parent's example and display of forgiveness will be a true beacon of truth to their children.

When your heart has been broken, your values trashed, and your authority mocked, it is a tall order not to take it personally. Parents with adolescents who challenge them must constantly pray for their kids during the storm. I would suggest a daily "heart check" to pull out any roots of resentment and bitterness and remember to forgive.

Forgiveness Begins at Home

Forgiveness in the parenting world is usually something that is passed down from parents to kids. This passing is displayed when a parent realizes that he or she has hurt someone within or outside the family relationships. Their example of asking someone for forgiveness and conveying genuine sorrow over something they did, something they didn't do, or some action that was misinterpreted is observed by their kids. It's another one of those monkey-see-monkey-do acts of asking forgiveness that restores relationships and allows for a new beginning after a rough patch of difficulties. This model is one that greatly impacts children of any age.

I don't think many kids pick up a concept of forgiveness unless they have parents who have asked for forgiveness for their shortcomings and hurting of others. I don't think that this can be taught—only caught by curious and attentive eyes that are watching every move when Mom and Dad have been offended.

Most parents know that telling their child to "say you're sorry" to another is really nothing more than a charade by kids to momentarily appease their parents who hope to teach the effect of inappropriate and hurtful actions. You should also know that these actions will cease when Mom and Dad are out of earshot or out of sight, and the same offense will happen again. It's the nature of kids.

We also know that most parents waiting for kids to say they're sorry for what they have done to them is sometimes nothing more than a self-absorbed tactic to restore the relationship to get what they want. Another word for this is *manipulation*. Most parents know when there is true heartfelt sorrow and when their child's actions are nothing more than self-centered pretense.

So parents must ask for forgiveness when they have hurt someone else, in hopes that their kids will pick up on this relationship-saving action and mimic this character trait in their own life.

When parents are hurt by their children's comments and actions and demand a sincere, heartfelt apology, I believe they are setting themselves up for a huge disappointment and hurt. And then if parents won't move beyond that hurt in the relationship with their child until their child recognizes their wrongdoing and apologizes for the actions, they're setting themselves up for nothing but frustration.

Forgiveness in the world of teens is something that is given. True forgiveness can't be forced, taken, manufactured, or coerced. It comes from the heart but does not come naturally. The ability for teens to acknowledge that they have hurt someone comes with age, wisdom, and the viewing of a good example. As a parent, your focus must be on giving forgiveness to those you have hurt. Change the expectation that your child will look at you and say, "Will you forgive me for what I've done?"—because you're not going to hear that often.

If I expected an apology every time a young person hurt or disappointed me, I would be one unhappy fellow. My role is to *give* forgiveness, expecting nothing from those who have hurt me. Forgiveness can never be demanded. I do to others what God has done for me. He doesn't allow my lack of repentance and forgiveness to get in the way of the relationship I have with Him. Parents would be wise to expect the same.

That's what is tough about having kids you love dearly when they move into their teen years. As you transition into a time of them practicing what they have been taught and making decisions about their life, you and I know that kids will make mistakes. And when they do, chances are that you will be the apex of that hurt.

It's hard to believe that the child you poured your life into and built a relationship with throughout the years would hurt you, sometimes intentionally but mostly unintentionally. To survive, it's important to change your expectations.

Changing Expectations

As the saying goes, "To err is human, to forgive is divine." In the world of parenting forgiveness, this is ever so true. The first four words depict the nature of an adolescent and teen-to-be, and the second four words accurately describe a parent trying to do the right thing as their child navigates through their teen years. Just as your parenting style shifts to a new mode for adolescence, your expectations for your child must shift as well. No longer is your child totally under your control. As you give them control of their life and allow them to make decisions, they will make mistakes. A change of expectations is in order.

Did you really think that you would never be hurt by your child in their quest for independence and their application of all they have been taught?

The teenage years are an age of testing, curiosity, exploration, searching for identity, processing truth, and looking at their culture with one eye cocked and their head a little tilted, wondering, "Where does this fit in?" It's also a time of confusion, conflict, and inconsistencies. And on top of it all, you're going to give them control and urge them to make more decisions in their life. Somewhere, they're going to violate your principles, make poor choices that appear to be a rejection of what you believe and want for your child, and do some things that might surprise you.

The tendency for any parent is to feel that their child is choosing to play on the opposing team rather than on yours. That's not always true. They're just trying to find out what their position is on the team they're playing on. Their bewilderment of the new playing field, coupled with their misperception of how their new culture fits into their world, is a bit overpowering. It will look like they're intentionally choosing to violate your standards, your beliefs, your ideals, and your morals. But I think they're just trying to put it all together.

To allow the pain of your child's struggle to interfere with your relationship with them only muddies the water for them. Expectations have to change or you will go crazy in the process, and you will ruin the relationship that you have greatly invested in.

Forgive and Forget

Here are some things I've learned about forgiveness when it comes to parenting teens.

Forgiveness is more about you offering forgiveness to your kids than them asking forgiveness from you. Plain and simple, you're going to have to ask for their forgiveness when you do something wrong to them, and not expect that they'll do the same when they wrong you. Whether it's looking past the hurt they cause in your life or learning not to let it affect you, you would be better off not expecting your child to come to you and say, "Mom, please forgive me for the way I treated you yesterday," or "Dad, I'm sorry for all the trouble I've caused this past year," or "I'm so sorry for the way I was disrespectful."

Don't let your child's lack of response for their wrongdoing and the hurt it caused to sidetrack you from the purpose of your parenting. You will be hurt along the way. I don't know many parents who haven't in some way felt the sting of a child's decisions, actions, or comments. This comes with the territory.

One day, perhaps, your child will recognize any challenges

and difficulties he or she has caused in your family. But until that day, spend more time demonstrating what it means to forgive.

Forgetting is essential. There was a young lady who lived with us at Heartlight who decided to leave the house she was living in and give me a piece of her mind about what she felt about living with us—including how she despised me and how much she hated being away from home. Her rant was intense. As I stood in the doorway of my home, she yelled, cursed, and was accusatory and irritable. My invitation for her to come inside was met with disrespect and anger. Every time I tried to get a word in edgewise, she interrupted me and took off on another rant about how terrible I was and how ineffective our program for kids was. I decided to just remain quiet and listen. She went on for thirty minutes. It seemed like hours.

At the end of her harsh outburst and when she felt like she had "spoken her mind" (what a drama queen she was!), she turned around and stormed back to the house where she was living. I was disturbed by her comments, and I walked back to our kitchen feeling like I had been verbally beat up. Deep down I felt hurt. Her words were vulgar, her intent was to damage me, and her comments were offensive.

Over the course of the next few months, I noticed that she was quiet around me. I sensed that she was embarrassed to be in my presence. I'm sure that as she was coming to an understanding of what she had done and realized how rude and improper her visit to my home was, she was a little ashamed. I wasn't sure she knew how to approach me.

Knowing that she wouldn't come to me, I decided to go toward her. It was my responsibility to make the first move. I wanted to let her know that her escapade at my home was forgiven and forgotten.

Here's what my conversation with her sounded like:

> **MARK**: "I want you to know that I don't think about or
> remember the time you came to my home."
> **JEN**: "You don't remember that?"
> **MARK**: "Remember what?"
> **JEN**: "Me crying and screaming and cussing at you at
> your front door."
> **MARK**: "You came to our door?"
> **JEN**: "Yes!"
> **MARK**: "Hmm, don't remember that."

I wanted her to know that I had forgotten about the whole interaction and didn't hold any of it against her. Not only was it forgiven, it was forgotten. And it was important for this reason. Bringing up the past eliminates, if not destroys, any element of hope for change in the future.

Bringing up the past eliminates hope. The past has an amazing way of clouding the future. So I don't ever bring it up. Sure, if there has been a pattern of behavior that is inappropriate, there needs to be a discussion about that habitual behavior. But it never does a parent good to bring up past events, decisions, and mistakes. Reminders of past mistakes only squelch the desire to make decisions, and they get in the way of relationships in eliminating the possibility of change.

There are two comments that can shut down a child and move him to believing that if he can never change what he's done in the past, then there's no hope for relationship in the future. Those statement are when you begin a sentence with "You always . . ." or "You never . . ."

And here's the killer. Whenever you tell your child, "You'll never change," it kills hope that anything will ever be different.

Mom and Dad, nothing goes unnoticed. The times your child hurts you in the course of applying the truth they've learned from you in this crazy, mixed-up world does not get lost in the chaos. God knows when your child has hurt you. He understands disappointment, so find your strength in Him, not your kids. And dedicate yourself to forgiving the hurt your children cause in your life so that your relationship with them can flourish.

To forgive is divine. Be to your children the loving parent God is to you.

>>> 20 <<<

Take a Regular Break

It's hard for any of us to walk into a setting where we know we're going to be criticized, isn't it? It's equally hard hearing that we should have done better, that we haven't performed up to our capabilities. And it's miserable to hear how we've disappointed those we love. Isn't that exactly what some tweens and teens experience every day—in school, in their social settings, and maybe even at home?

I encourage parents to step into their adolescents' shoes and think about how hard it is to come home every day from doing their best not to get sucked into the cultural whirlpool, only to hear once again from their parents how they're not doing enough or doing it right.

Have you ever wondered why kids can't wait to go hang out with friends, or become engrossed with a boyfriend or girlfriend, or hang out with the bad kids you don't want your child hanging with? It's more than just socialization. I think they're looking for *rest.*

Have you scratched your head in your own curiosity wondering about teens who are consumed with media and video games or love to watch movies, read books, and get lost in fantasy? I think they're looking for a *getaway.*

Have you been somewhat puzzled by the number of kids who smoke pot, get drunk on the weekends, don't have any motivation, or don't care about much? Sadly, many are looking for an *escape* from the pressures they experience in a culture that is counter to how they have been raised. While I don't agree with their behavior, I sure understand it.

Has it surprised you that so many college kids want to go spend time on the mission field abroad when there are mission fields in their own backyard? I've had many teens and twenty-somethings tell me that the lure of mission work had more to do with them wanting to travel, take a break, and looking for exhilaration than desiring to be a missionary for a couple of weeks.

Most kids I know are looking for a place to have fun, to have a little excitement, and to have rest. My hope is that your home can become a place that provides an atmosphere of relationship that allows for fun, engages in something that is exiting, and provides a place of rest for your kids, a retreat from the pressures of their life.

Here's what I think is happening with kids today in their teen years. It is especially important for parents of kids of all ages to understand the world their child will live in during their adolescent years as they give their child more control, more choices, more freedom and independence, and more opportunity to practice what has been preached. When parents lack this understanding and don't have a concept of the need of rest, kids find it elsewhere, outside the home. An understanding of what you're up against may motivate you all the more to be more precise in the training of your child.

Alexa was a young lady who came from a good home, a great family, was involved in church and her youth group, and had plenty of opportunities before her—truly the all-American kid. Sometime during her junior year in high school everything changed. Her candid response to my simple question of "What happened?" didn't surprise me. She answered, "I used to be a good kid, but I got bored, I got tired, I got worn out and it just seemed that I could never do anything right, so I quit. It was too much work, and I felt like I was swimming upstream all day, only to come home and battle with my parents about why I wasn't doing better."

As time gets tight at home with everyone busier and life increasingly ticking at a faster pace with more activities, more commitments, and fuller schedules, the amount of time dedicated to correcting problems tends to remain the same. What gets squeezed out is the relational time. The verbal correcting of misdoings, shortcomings, and inappropriate behavior becomes priority to such a level that so much time and effort is spent "correcting" that there's very little time for "connecting."

A Place Where They Feel Safe

In a child's eyes upon entering the teen years, home can be viewed as a battlefield and a place where "rest" never happens. They come home from school, where they have worked hard to maintain the standard, uphold the principles, and stand for what is right against a tsunami of influence that is pushing against them telling them to be this, accept this lifestyle, try this stuff, look different, listen to this, say that, believe it all, don't listen to your parents . . . whew! Upon getting home they are pushed to clean their room, do their chores, feed the dog, study for an hour, get ready for piano, go to gymnastics, go to church, blah, blah, blah, blah. They are worn out! They need a break. They need rest. And if parents don't give it to them, teenagers will find ways to relieve the pressure that the world's influence is putting on them.

Parents must be intentional about creating a place of rest. What teens face today compared with what you and I faced during our teenage years is hardly comparable. Many times the battle of expectations at home feels harder to a teen than the cultural war that is trying to drown him. Everybody needs a break from the battles of life, and teens are no exception.

Kaylee told me that she dreaded going home every day after school. Everyone at school knew her as the good girl, but the minute she stepped into her home the battle began. She shared how she was never wearing the right thing, that she was told to stay at home rather than get with friends, and she needed to be with family after a day of hanging with her friends. She was told to study and then come to dinner, where she was grilled about how she was doing in her walk with Christ. She didn't feel her parents listened to her, so she shut down. She said she couldn't give an answer that would pacify them, and everything she commented on was never right. She said the only time she felt rest was when she would drink from a secret bottle of alcohol that would put her to sleep and give her the rest she needed.

Jake came home only to be reminded that his room was dirty, that he wasn't on time, that he needed to study more, he needed to go to youth group, he should have done this, he shouldn't have done that, and he ought to do better. He said that every time his dad opened his mouth, he wondered what he would say next about what Jake was doing wrong. He said that the only time he felt comfortable and at rest was when he smoked pot with his girlfriend. He described the feeling he got the first time he smoked pot, saying, "It was the first time I felt normal."

Both Kaylee's and Jake's parents told me they were just normal kids up until their junior year in high school, and all of a sudden things changed. I really don't think either parent realized what they were doing until their child was finally pushed over the edge and searched for the rest they needed when it couldn't be found at home.

My point is this: constant condemnation and correction will push a child to find another place of rest. They will find it somewhere. My hope is that they'll find it at your home.

Here are some suggestions to help make your home a place where they'll find some of those things that they desperately need and for which they are searching.

A Place Where They Can Rest

Would you say that your home is a place of rest? Would your spouse say that your home is restful? Would your kids say that the atmosphere around the home is one where all can relax and have some downtime? Ask them. And continue to ask them that question every few months to make sure your home is a respite from the craziness of life. Here are some other questions to consider:

- Do you have a day at your home that everyone can rest, recover, and be refreshed?
- Do you allow your kids to sleep in and catch up on their rest on weekends and holidays?
- Do you allow your kids the opportunity to do nothing at times?
- When is the last time your family had a relaxing night at home?

This doesn't mean that you relax the boundaries and forget the rules that have been established in your home. You can allow some downtime within those boundaries by relaxing some expectations of cleanliness, tidiness, doing chores, sitting around and watching sports or movies. Even type A personalities need time to stop and recharge their batteries.

A Place Where They Feel Connected

I'm convinced of this: you're going to spend your money. And you'll spend money on your kids. What you don't spend, you'll give to your kids. So give it to them in a way of creating connections during their teenage years when they need it the most.

A man recently came up to me at a speaking engagement and told me he had heard me speak a couple of years earlier, when I encouraged families to reconsider how they spend their money. I tell families to quit saving all the time and start investing—investing in the life of your child. He shared with me how they spent some savings and bought a sailboat. He continued to tell me how they've hauled that sailboat to the Gulf of Mexico, to the lakes of Michigan, and to bodies of water he never knew existed, all the while camping and creating memories with his kids that they will never forget. He said this. "We couldn't afford to, but we couldn't afford not to."

Kids are looking for connections. And what better connections to make than those with your own kids? Here's another idea.

Have a weekly joke night at your home. Tell everyone that they must come to the table and bring a clean joke they found on the Internet. The purpose is to make others laugh. A family that laughs together . . . has a good time. And don't always make something spiritual out of it. Relax, have a good time, and make sure your kids go to bed at night saying, "I had a good time with my parents tonight."

During your child's adolescent years, invest your time making connections with them. Tell others that you won't be volunteering, teaching classes, leading small groups, serving at the church, leading Boy Scouts or Girl Scouts, or serving on boards. Tell them that you are taking a break to spend time with someone in your family who won't be with you much longer. The teenage years go quickly, and before you know it, your child will be moving out. So take advantage of the time now, so that you have a great relationship in the future, one filled with memories of how Mom and Dad gave their all for their kids.

And once the kids are grown and living on their own, busy yourself in all those other activities. The lessons that you've learned from and about your kids need to be passed on to others.

A Place Where They're Not Corrected All the Time

If you have the constant tendency to correct and criticize your child, whether they are a tween or a teen, you might want to rethink the type of atmosphere you are creating for your child as he or she walks through the adolescent years. Consider this. Only correct your kids on Tuesday, Thursday, and Saturday. Don't do any major correction for them on the other days.

This will force you to choose only the important things to correct and keep you from being a nag, or one who is always picking at their inconsistencies and inconsideration. They may do things wrong, and if they violate the boundaries and rules of your home, then yes, there will have to be consequences. That's of their own choosing.

You have a choice of determining whether you create an atmosphere of relationship and connection, or an atmosphere where they seek rest elsewhere. It's up to you.

Take a break. You'll see a change in them . . . and you might just feel better about your own self as well.

>>> Conclusion <<<

Family—The Permanent Harbor in a Constant Storm

Every Christmas we spread out a thousand-piece jigsaw puzzle on a table and begin the arduous and focused task of trying to put a menagerie of odd-shaped and multicolored pieces together to match the image on the front of the box.

While the adults are busy adding their geometric conceptualized placement of pieces or their color spectrum complement, my two granddaughters are in the other room putting together their twenty-four-piece puzzle, which takes about five minutes. I've often wondered why we adults just don't opt for the smaller puzzle, bypass all the confusion, conflict, clashing of pieces, and avoid this challenging ordeal designed to amuse and present hardships that for the most part, can only be solved by ingenuity, patient effort, and focused attention.

Maybe it's the challenge. Maybe it's because we see the bigger picture on the manufacturer's box and want to recreate the same on our table. Perhaps it's the enjoyment of doing something together. Maybe it's what happens along the way in pursuit of a focused effort. Maybe it's just the knowledge that you're piecing something together that is much more than just that area of the puzzle you're working on. Who knows? Maybe everyone has a different motive—a different reason to assemble this jumbled mess of odd-shaped pieces into a masterpiece.

I've seen where some people (odd ones to me) glue their finished puzzle together and shellac the front to hold the pieces and hide the lines, and then hang it on their wall. That seems odd to me as well. A puzzle on display for all to see that says, "Look what I did; maybe you can do it as well!" is just weird to me. Hey, different strokes for different folks.

For me, the joy is in the journey. That's why about five minutes after it's finished, I take apart the puzzle and toss the pieces back into the box, only to take it out a few years later when I have a hankerin' to feel challenged again.

It's interesting to me how people put together a jigsaw puzzle. Some do it by colors. Some do it by size and shape. Some have to constantly look at the bigger picture. Others just do it by feel, and some do it by mimicking the box picture and put pieces in places where they currently don't fit, but eventually will.

I know that many times thoughts have crossed my mind in piecing together a perplexing puzzle that are spoken out of frustration and anger. Comments like . . .

- "This piece doesn't fit anywhere!"
- "The manufacturer must have left out some pieces."
- "Someone has lost some pieces and we won't be able to finish!"
- "This doesn't work!"
- "Did some buffoon combine two puzzles here?"
- "I think I'm going to quit . . . This is taking too much time."
- "Do I need help? Are you kidding? I can do this myself."

Every year, I say the same things. Now, deep down in my puzzle memory bank, I know the picture will come together, even though I'm not sure how it's all going to fit.

Puzzling through the Parenting Years

Putting together a puzzle is a lot like parenting. Most parents spend the first twelve years of a child's life assembling the corner pieces by building the boundaries, and then they start filling in the picture with what is familiar. They spend the next six to ten years tackling the unknown colors and pieces, trying to figure out where they go and how they all fit. The challenge is usually the latter, not the former.

But here's another, essential part of the parenting puzzle. If you don't understand this, you might just have the tendency to delay the finishing of your puzzle to a later time. This part has to do with the colors.

Simply put, if it were not for the dark and jagged pieces that seemingly have no purpose, the puzzle would not become the masterpiece it was created to be. The dark pieces are just as much a part of the puzzle as the brightly colored and rounded pieces, as their complementary relationship with one another highlights and accents the bigger picture's beauty.

If you're putting together a puzzle, you know what I'm talking about. Regardless of where you are in putting together your puzzling puzzle, one day, after building boundaries, piecing together the familiar, and handling the dark areas as well as the lighter areas, you'll be able to say, "Now I see how it all fits together!"

This book has been geared toward helping parents have a better relationship with teenagers, who desperately need them to communicate the message, "There is nothing you can do to make me love you more, and there is nothing you can do to make me love you less." Parents need to be the permanent harbor in the midst of the stormy waters of the culture that their children are trying to navigate.

By extending a hand of relationship to your child rather than exercising the arm of authority, most parents will find an amicable and workable relationship with their adolescents. Teens change because of relationship, not because of authority. As they change, my challenge to parents is be involved, active, and engaged in the life of their children.

Chances are those kids you're pouring your life into will be around a long time. And chances are they'll usher in a whole new world of grandparenting, which is well worth the investment in your own kids. And the greater chances are that between you and your kids, one of you will bury the other. The relationship you have with your kids is probably the most important relationship that you have next to your marriage. You may struggle through some of those "dark pieces" of the puzzle of life and find that what you thought was bad really turned out to be good, and what you thought was awful created an amazing way for your kids (and you) to learn a lesson that would have never been taught any other way.

Your Kids Need You!

Because of the big-picture plan for your family, I encourage you to invest your time, effort, and resources into the relationships around you that count, and not to get bogged down in minor stuff that will eventually pass in time. Your kids are faced with things that you and I never thought would even exist. And they're exposed to things that most of us didn't get exposed to until much later in life. The confusion of media bombardment, gender issues, and living in a time of uncertainty all have a tendency to pull your kids away from you in their preteen and teenage years. They need you to help them get through their confusion and mature into healthy adults.

It sounds like it's going to be a hard trek, doesn't it? While I believe that if we're not involved in the life of our kids that they'll surely have a tough time, I do believe that there's hope and opportunity to raise good kids who are responsible, mature, and motivated for the challenges of adulthood that lie ahead.

By utilizing the same styles and techniques that I use in my work with teens, I truly believe parents can offer their kids something they'll never get anywhere else—that's a relationship with you that provides a connection that is unlike any other.

The time that you spend with your child is essential to having success in their teen years. That's why I encourage these weekly one-on-one meetings, whether it's to ask questions or to make the most of conflict, to give your kids opportunity to get to know you in a way that shares life during their adolescent years.

So as you launch into the world of teens, remember to start shifting the way that you talk with your child and ask more questions. Look at the next few years as opportunities to help your child put into place all those things he or she has learned and start trusting your teen to take control of his or her life. Help your child become independent through encouragement, and subtract strictness which only discourages.

Forgive much, laugh more often, give freedom to make mistakes and pick your battles wisely, and I'm sure that you'll do well.

Your Drama Queen and Tough Guy Are Worth It

Your drama queen and tough guy are worth your investment of your life, even when you don't understand where a certain piece of the puzzle fits.

I'm convinced of this: you are just as much a part of their puzzle as they are of yours. There are many puzzles on the table within your family, and their uniqueness is as exceptional and exclusive as a falling snowflake or your unique fingerprints.

May your family be blessed as you parent your children through their teenage years. I'm sure one day you'll laugh at the antics of your drama queen. And you'll marvel at your tough guy as he finishes his chapter of adolescence and moves into adulthood.

In the process, enjoy the puzzle!

>>> Appendix A <<<

Conversation Starters

Here are some questions to start a conversation with your teenager (see chapter 11). Remember, ask the question and don't give an answer unless they ask you. And don't share your opinion about their answer; their answers will give you insight into their life. Don't do anything to shut down their response. These are great for around the table discussions, while you're riding in the car, or traveling together.

- What's something about our family that sticks out the most in your mind?
- If you could change one thing about yourself, what would it be?
- If you could change one thing about our family, what would it be?
- If you could change one thing about me, what would it be?
- What causes the most fear in your life?
- What's the most fun thing you've ever done?
- Am I really as bad as you think I am?
- Do you think that we're the only people out of all the solar systems known to man?
- What would be one thing that I could do for you to make your life better?

- If there were one person in the world that you wish would give you a call, who would it be and what do you think you'd talk about?
- We're all known for something. What would you like to be known for?
- Do you find yourself doing things that you don't want to do, and not doing the things you want to do?
- What would someone in your class who doesn't know you say about you after watching you?
- Who is the most talented musician you've ever heard? Do you think you'll be listening to him or her ten years from now?
- Do you think all people have the capability of being famous?
- Do you think that you'll be famous one day? If so, what for? If not, why not?
- Do you think dogs hear everything we say and hide their feelings well, or do they see us at our worst, and just decide to love us anyway?
- When is a friend a real friend, and when is one not?
- How many times have you been hurt this past month? What was it that hurt the most?
- What one word would you use to describe our family?
- If you won the lotto jackpot, and had to spend it all, what would you spend it on?
- Out of all the teachers you've ever had, which one do you remember the most, and why?
- What talent would you like to have that you don't?
- How much money would you have to be given to shave your head?

- Do you think everyone on *American Idol* is really that good?
- Are you more likely to talk on your phone or send texts?
- What do you think it means to have a spirit of excellence in the way you work?
- What's the weirdest thing that you've ever seen on the Internet?
- What do you think the perfect woman would look like?
- What's the coolest looking mustache you've ever seen?
- If you could spend one week on vacation at a place of your choice and you could take one person with you, where would it be and who would you take?
- When was the last time you laughed out loud, and what made you laugh?
- If you could sit down and eat a meal with one person in the world, who would it be?
- Do you ever have a hard time taking what you know to be true into the world that you live in?
- Who's the weirdest person you know? Is there anything about this person that is just like you?
- What would be the first thing you'd do if the sun didn't come up tomorrow?
- What do you think is the biggest controversy happening in the world today?
- Do you think that you're too fat, too tall, too skinny, too short, or have the wrong color hair?
- Is there a disease you would never want to die from?
- If you were an animal, what kind of animal would you want to be? Why?
- Who's the greatest sports hero of all time?

- Do you think it's important to always have to share your opinion, and what do you think of people who do?
- What's the neatest website you've ever visited?
- Do you think the music you listen to influences you, or is it just an expression of what you feel?
- Which is better: having a great family or having a lot of money?
- Who's your closest friend, and what one wish would you wish for that friend?
- Why do you think that just about all men on television sitcoms are portrayed as buffoons?
- Do you think that you would talk more if you texted less?
- Do you think that Facebook is true to life, or is it a little fake? What one word would you use to describe people who are always on Facebook?
- What would make school mean more to you?
- If a tornado was coming toward your home and you had only time to grab one thing before you protected yourself in a cellar, what would you take?
- What's your favorite movie of all time? What's so special about it?
- Would you rather be rich and have as much money as you'll ever need, or have everyone think you're the kindest and most helpful person they've ever met?
- What is the favorite meal of the person sitting next to you?
- Would you rather travel across country in a covered wagon or fly around the universe in a space shuttle?
- Do you have a special talent that others don't know about?
- Who is your best friend and why?
- What's the funniest joke you've ever heard? Will you tell it?

- What is the worst food you've ever eaten at school?
- Do you think there are people in the world that have never made a mistake?
- Would you ever jump out of an airplane with a parachute or hop off a bridge on a bungee rope?
- Do you remember where you were when you heard of the greatest tragedy? What was the tragedy, and what were you doing when you heard the news?
- What do you miss the most about <insert name of someone he or she knows who has died>?
- How is this year in school different from your last year in school?
- What actor or actress would you like to be like?
- What do you think is the greatest thing that's ever been done? What is the greatest thing that *you've* ever done?
- Which are better: tattoos or piercings?
- What's a lesson about life that you've learned this week?
- If you could have plastic surgery on one part of your body, what would it be and why?
- If you could see someone in concert and sit on the first row, who would it be?
- When you hear someone talk about a "real man," who comes to your mind?

>>> Appendix B <<<

How to Discuss Conflict

The goal of investing one week's time into a one-on-one
weekly meeting with your child is to create a place, time,
and opportunity for you and your child to discuss any conflict, potential or current. These are some discussion starters:

- Sweetheart, your mom and I don't think its time for you to
  get a cell phone just yet. I know others in your class have
  them. You're thirteen, and we've always said that you can
  have one when you're fifteen. I'm willing to back that up to
  fourteen. Is that a good compromise for you?
- Your dad and I think that it's best that you not spend the
  night at your friend's house yet. He's more than welcome
  to come here for the night, but we're not comfortable with
  you there until we meet his parents. Do you think they
  would call us or we could drop by to meet them sometime?
- I see some things that concern me about your use of the
  Internet. I looked at the Internet history and see that you've
  been spending some time on some porn sites that aren't
  appropriate. Let's figure out what to do to make sure this
  doesn't become a problem.
- I think you and I disagree on something that's important
  to talk about. It's about the amount of time you spend

playing video games. It seems like that's all you want to do, and you seem to be spending more time playing than we agree to. Let's talk about what solutions we can find to this problem. Do you think it's a problem?

- I'm struggling with the way you treat your mom. For the most part, it seems like you're mad at her all the time and treat her with a great deal of disrespect. Let's talk about what Mom's doing wrong in her approach to you, and then let's talk about what you're doing wrong in your approach to her. I love your mom, and I know you do too. Do you think we can come to some agreement on how we're going to live respectfully together in our home?

- I'm not sure of this one friend of yours. It seems as though every time you're with her, you get in trouble at school, or when you two get together, you start to be negative. Now, I don't want to pick your friends for you, but I also don't want you to get in trouble at school or become negative. We want to get to know her better. Could she come over for dinner and let us get to know her?

- I've spent some time thinking about what we talked about last week. Considering what you said, what your mom has told me, and the conclusion I've come to, we're not going to let you go on the spring break trip you ask us about. Unless you can convince me otherwise this morning, I'm going to have to stick with my decision. So give it your best shot, and let's see if you can get me to change my mind.

- Is there anything that's happening now that you think might be a conflict between us in the future? Your mom heard some things, and I checked them out with some other parents, and they've all said the same thing. Anything you think we need to talk about this morning?

- I know that we've set the rules at home and you're having a tough time with a couple of them. Let's talk about those. But first, do you understand the reason we've set up these rules for our home? Then, is there a reason that you're having a tough time following them?

- Hey, you're almost eighteen. How can I help you make this next transition in life without wrecking the way we operate in our home.

- I want to be the kind of father (or mother) you want me to be. I'm not sure that I understand what that looks like, and I'm not sure how to get there, but I would love to discuss this and not be afraid to make changes. You game to talk about this?

- Look, I know you want to finish the eighth grade and move on to high school. I also know that the way you're headed, that just isn't going to happen. Let's talk about what I can do to help you accomplish what you want. Can we do that?

- You've been playing soccer for the last five years, and it sure seems that you've loved it. Help me understand why you want to give it up now, after you've committed to play this next year.

- I know that your sister (brother) can drive you nuts. I had a brother (sister) like that that when I was growing up. And just as my brother has turned out to be a pretty good guy, I'm sure your sister will also. I just want to make sure that you don't kill each other before you have the chance to turn out to be pretty good, as well. What can I do to ensure that the fighting stops so that there can be some harmony in our home?

- You know that I can't stand your music. You also know that I'm not going to play music police—not one of the things that I signed up for when becoming a parent. So, I'm giving you this iPod with ear buds so you can keep your music to yourself in hopes that my migraines will stop. Can you help me not die prematurely by not blaring your music through the house?

- You know your mother and I don't get along well. And she dislikes me more since I got remarried. But she is your mother, and I'm asking you to not take out your anger towards me on her. She's trying the best she can. Can you help her in her house and can you promise to discuss with me any anger that you have for me?

- I blew it and made a huge mistake. And I want to say I'm sorry for what I've done and I want to ask you to forgive me. Is there anything I can do to make our relationship right? I want to have a good relationship; I'm tired of not getting along.

Notes

Introduction: What Duck Hunting Taught Me about Adolescence

1. See www.heartlightministries.org for more information about Heartlight Ministries.

Chapter 1: Overexposure to Everything

1. Nick Bontis, *Information Bombardment: Rising Above the Digital Onslaught* (Ontario, Canada: Institute for Intellectual Capital Research, 2011).
2. Facebook Statistics, http://www.facebook.com/press/info .php?statistics.
3. Family Safe Media, "Pornography Statistics," http://www .familysafemedia.com/pornography_statistics.html.
4. Reelso Online Video Marketing Guide, April 2010.
5. Play Station Universe, "http://www.psu.com/forums/showthread .php/18716-69-of-American-Heads-of-Households-play-video-g
6. Anjani Chandra, William D. Mosher, Casey Copen, and Catlainn Slonean, "Sexual Behavior, Sexual Attraction, and Sexual Identity in the United States: Data from the 2006–2008 National Survey of Family Growth," *National Health Statistics Report*,; no 36. (Hyattsville, MD: National Center for Health Statistics. 2011), Tables 5–6.
7. Laura Duberstein Lindberg, Rachel Jones, and John S. Santelli, "Noncoital Sexual Activities Among Adolescents," *Journal of Adolescent Health* 43(3): 231–38.
8. Chandra et al, "Sexual Behavior," Table 7.

Chapter 2: Lack of Real Connection

1. Don Reisinger, "6.1 Trillion Text Messages to be Sent in 2010,"

CNET, October 19, 2010, http://news.cnet.com/8301-13506_3
-20020101-17.html.
2. Amanda Lenhart, "Teens, Cell Phones and Texting," Pew
Research Center, April 20, 2010, http://pewresearch.org
/pubs/1572/teens-cell-phones-text-messages.
3. Richard Morin, "What Teens Really Think," *The Washington
Post,* October 23, 2005, http://www.highbeam.com/
doc/1P2-81115.html.

Chapter 5: Loss of Gender Differences

1. Catherine Rampell, "Women Now a Majority in American
Workplaces," *New York Times,* February 5, 2010, http://www
.nytimes.com/2010/02/06/business/economy/06women.html.

Chapter 16: Pick Your Battles Wisely

1. Y. T. Uhls and P. M. Greenfield, "The Rise of Fame: An
Historical Content Analysis," *Cyberpsychology: Journal of
Psychosocial Research on Cyberspace* 5(1): article 1.

Chapter 18: Offer Freedom to Make Mistakes

1. Janice Hoffman, *Relationship Rules: 12 Strategies for Creating a
Love That Lasts* (Venus, FL: Venus Publishing, 2007).

About the Author

Mark Gregston is the founder and executive director of Heartlight, a residential counseling center for teens located in Longview, Texas, where he lives with sixty high school kids from around the country. He is also the host of *Parenting Today's Teens*, a daily and weekend radio program heard on over fourteen hundred radio outlets, helping parents across North America navigate through the turbulent waters of their child's adolescence. He is a popular speaker and author, combining humor and stories with insights and wisdom gained from his thirty-eight years of working with teens and parents, and spends almost every weekend of the year leading a parenting seminar in various cities.

Mark has been married for thirty-eight years to his high school sweetheart, Jan, who has tolerated his crazy schedule of working with kids. They have two kids, three grand kids, one dog, one cat, four llamas, and way too many horses.